OXFORD PLAYSCRIPTS

CRY THE BELOVED COUNTRY

Alan Paton

adapted by Roy Sargeant

OXFORD
UNIVERSITY PRESS

UNIVERSITY PRESS

Great Clarendon Street, Oxford OX2 6DP

Oxford University Press is a department of the University of Oxford.
It furthers the University's objective of excellence in research,
scholarship, and education by publishing worldwide in

Oxford   New York

Auckland   Cape Town   Dar es Salaam   Hong Kong   Karachi
Kuala Lumpur   Madrid   Melbourne   Mexico City   Nairobi
New Delhi   Shanghai   Taipei   Toronto

With offices in

Argentina   Austria   Brazil   Chile   Czech Republic   France   Greece
Guatemala   Hungary   Italy   Japan   Poland   Portugal   Singapore
South Korea   Switzerland   Thailand   Turkey   Ukraine   Vietnam

Oxford is a registered trade mark of Oxford University Press
in the UK and in certain other countries

Adapted from *Cry, the Beloved Country: the play* © Roy Sargeant and
Oxford University Press Southern Africa (Pty) Ltd 2006

This edition is published by arrangement with Oxford University Press
Southern Africa (Pty) Ltd (for sale throughout the United Kingdom and
not for export therefrom)

Activity section © Oxford University Press 2008

The moral rights of the author have been asserted

Database right Oxford University Press (maker)

First published in 2008

All rights reserved. No part of this publication may be reproduced,
stored in a retrieval system, or transmitted, in any form or by any means,
without the prior permission in writing of Oxford University Press, or as
expressly permitted by law, or under terms agreed with the appropriate
reprographics rights organization. Enquiries concerning reproduction
outside the scope of the above should be sent to the Rights Department,
Oxford University Press, at the address above

You must not circulate this book in any other binding or cover
and you must impose this same condition on any acquirer

All rights whatsoever in this play are strictly reserved and application
for performance should strictly be made for commencement of
rehearsal to: Rights Department, Education Division, Oxford University
Press, Great Clarendon Street, Oxford, OX2 6DP. No performance may
be made unless a licence has been obtained and no alterations may be
made on the title or the text of the play without the author's prior
written consent.

British Library Cataloguing in Publication Data

Data available

ISBN 978 0 19 8326953

10 9 8

Typeset by Palimpsest Book Production Ltd, Grangemouth, Stirlingshire.
Printed in Great Britain by CPI Group (UK) Ltd., Croydon CR0 4YY

Acknowledgements

Cover Imagery © Hoberman Collection/Corbis
Artwork is by Neil Chapman/Beehive Illustration

The Publisher would like to thank Jenny Roberts for writing the Activities section.

CONTENTS

GENERAL INTRODUCTION	4
WHAT THE ADAPTER SAYS	5
CAST AND COMPANY	7
THE PLAY	11
GLOSSARY	103
ACTIVITIES	107

GENERAL INTRODUCTION

With a fresh, modern look, this classroom-friendly series boasts an exciting range of authors – from Pratchett to Chaucer – whose works have been expertly adapted by such well-known and popular writers as Philip Pullman and David Calcutt.

Many teachers use OXFORD *Playscripts* to study the format, style, and structure of playscripts with their students; for speaking and listening assignments; to initiate discussion of relevant issues in class; to cover Drama as part of the curriculum; as an introduction to the novel of the same title; and to introduce the less able or willing to pre-1914 literature.

At the back of each OXFORD *Playscript*, you will find a brand new Activity section, which not only addresses the points above, but also features close text analysis, and activities that provide support for underachieving readers and act as a springboard for personal writing.

Many schools will simply read through the play in class with no staging at all, and the Activity sections have been written with this in mind, with individual activities ranging from debates and designing campaign posters to writing extra scenes or converting parts of the original novels into playscript form.

For those of you, however, who do wish to take to the stage, each OXFORD *Playscript* also features 'A Note on Staging' – a section dedicated to suggesting ways of staging the play, as well as examining the props and sets you may wish to use.

Above all, we hope you will enjoy using OXFORD *Playscripts*, be it on the stage or in the classroom.

WHAT THE ADAPTER SAYS

It was in 2003, the centenary of Alan Paton's birth, that I conceived the idea of doing a play adaptation of his first novel *Cry, the Beloved Country*, a deeply moving and emotional read.

In 1946, after ten years heading a Reformatory for black boys, Paton became more and more involved with the plight of black South Africans, their poverty, the deprivation they suffered in so many critical ways as compared with the comforts and affluence of white South Africa.

So, I was concerned in doing the adaptation to re-represent what most occupies Paton's mind in the novel: the conflict between man and society. In his autobiography, Paton talks of this conflict as the 'ultimate conflict'. As the narrative of the novel unfolds, Paton never loses sight of his central thematic concern: to demonstrate how in the hearts of men (in *Cry*, the hearts of Stephen Kumalo and James Jarvis), who are concerned with the just ordering of an unjust society, two 'irreconcilable moral concepts are in conflict . . . The one is the sanctity of life, the other the duty of compassion.'

There is violence in *Cry*, both graphic and implied. But it is not the violence you remember as the story ends. It is hope, faith, charity and, above all, love that haunt your mind, powered as they are by the extraordinary reconciliation between black priest and white farmer with which the story ends. Setting about the adaptation, I was determined that these issues would be captured in the play with absolute clarity.

Adapting a novel which teems with characters (I counted them in *Cry*: 138) makes one essential demand of the adapter: what are you going to leave out? I knew the play would run for about three hours and I knew it could not run any longer being keenly aware of the South African audiences' ability to concentrate. I felt, therefore, that care had to be taken with what sub-plots should be drawn in from the novel. And so I decided that the stories of two fathers and two sons had to be my focus. This resulted in abandoning totally the story of the Reverend Kumalo's sister, Gertrude, for example.

Gertrude had, like many black people in the mid-1940s, left her rural village in Natal and gone to Johannesburg, place of gold, to find a better life. She had been followed by her nephew, Absalom, Kumalo's son. Gertrude falls on hard times in Johannesburg and that is the reason Kumalo travels there and, in the novel, he becomes involved in two searches, one for his sister and later the other for his son. This could not be in the play and so the play focuses tightly on the plight of Absalom only, the story with which the novel climaxes.

For actors there is a rich mine to be excavated in terms of characterization by delving into the novel. I just want to say one important word about the dialogue. It is as

Paton wrote it in the novel. First of all he had a keen ear for the way people spoke in the 1940s, especially white men, with their formal and cryptic manner of speech, as demonstrated by their use of surnames when addressing each other. But then there is the near-poetic manner of speech of the black characters. This must not be tampered with because it is important to understand that Paton was hearing Zulu being spoken in his head when he wrote this dialogue and he 'translated' it, as it were, into the English you read on the page.

In imagining the stage world of the play my mind turned to the epic plays of Berthold Brecht. Obviously, the action of *Cry* crosses a wide geography – from Ixopo in Natal, by train to Johannesburg, round and round the suburbs and townships of the Place of Gold, back to Ixopo, the village and the Jarvis farm – interiors, exteriors tumbling one upon the other.

Brecht's dictum about theatre design was in my mind all the time I was doing the adaptation: only put on stage 'significant statements about reality'. So, in my imagination I saw, above all the 'lovely road' as mentioned in the first line of the novel, dominating the stage setting with other areas spreading off to stage left and stage right that could be used for interiors or other areas of action. The action of the play must follow hard-upon, one scene flowing seamlessly into the next. There must be no interruptions.

I gave Alan Paton a place onstage, not just at the beginning and the end in person, but by using prose narrative links from the novel. Once again the use of various narrators will be recognized as a Brechtian device.

As I worked I found that 14 main characters and 13 actors could tell the story, with much doubling, trebling of roles and ensemble playing, so that in the play the 138 characters in the novel could be pared down to some 38. Again, visually Brecht is the guide, simple changes of costume, a head scarf here, a priest's biretta there.

The 'book ending' of the adaptation with, at the beginning, the voice of Alan Paton speaking the first lovely lines of the novel and then, at the end, being seen on screen reading the last bleakly hopeful paragraph of the book proved hugely effective in the staging. And the ideas of the use of tape and video prompted the brilliant first director of the play, Heinrich Reisenhofer, to present the murder of Arthur Jarvis by Absalom Kumalo on video as well.

When I produced the film adaptation of Athol Fugard's play *The Road to Mecca*, I recall Fugard's remark after seeing the movie for the first time. His comment was simple and telling, 'Yes,' he said, 'I recognize the same experience as in the theatre.' I hope that in reading or seeing the play of *Cry, the Beloved Country* readers and audiences will identify the same experience as that presented by the novel.

Roy Sargeant

CAST AND COMPANY

The play was first produced by Artscape and Roy Sargeant Productions and opened at the National Arts Festival, Grahamstown, South Africa, on 27 June 2003 and at the Artscape Theatre, Cape Town, on 8 July 2003. The production then toured to Bloemfontein, Durban and Oudtshoorn. It had the following cast:

THE CAST

The Kumalo family
REV. STEPHEN KUMALO — JOKO SCOTT
HIS WIFE — THOBEKA MAQHUTYANA
ABSALOM, their son — MORENA MEDI
GIRL, Absalom's wife — NKULI SIBEKO
JOHN KUMALO, Stephen's brother — WISEMAN SITHOLE
MATTHEW, his son — CHRIS GXALABA

The Jarvis family
JAMES JARVIS — DAVID MULLER
MARGARET, his wife — ADRIENNE PEARCE
ARTHUR, their son — LEON LIEBENBERG
BOY, Arthur's son — JOHAN VERMAAK

Friends of the family
REV. THEOPHILUS MSIMANGU — NHLANHLA MAVUNDLA
FATHER VINCENT — MATTHEW WILD
MR HARRISON — ROGER DWYER

Contemporary schoolboy — JOHAN VERMAAK

All other roles played by the Company.
(For suggested role allocation see below and on the next two pages.)

The play takes place in 1946 in what was then the Union of South Africa, in Ndotsheni and Carisbrooke in the southern, rural area of Natal, and in the city of Johannesburg.

Play was directed by Heinrich Reisenhofer

Designed by Peter Cazalet

Lighting designed by Kobus Rossouw

THE COMPANY

Five black male actors
Five white male actors
Two black female actors
One white female actor

Actor 1	Stephen Kumalo
Actor 2	Passenger on train to Johannesburg
	Mr Dubula
	Matthew Kumalo
	Napoleon Letsitsi
Actor 3	Young Man who cons Stephen
	Absalom Kumalo
Actor 4	Theophilus Msimangu
	Villager
Actor 5	Stephen's Wife
	Mrs Mkize
Actor 6	Mr Mafolo, man at the bus station
	John Kumalo

	Native Servant
	Kuluse, a Villager
Actor 7	Arthur Jarvis
	Prison Warder
	Clerk of the Court
	Villager
	Prison Official
Actor 8	Mrs Ndlela
	John Kumalo's 'Wife'
	Girl
Actor 9	Margaret Jarvis
	Barbara Smith
Actor 10	Father Vincent
	Police Captain
	Prosecutor
	Villager
Actor 11	Mr de Villiers
	John Harrison
	Judge
	Villager
Actor 12	James Jarvis
Actor 13	Contemporary Schoolboy
	Boy, Arthur Jarvis's son

Commuters at the station in Pietermaritzburg
Passengers on the train to Johannesburg
Bus passengers who will not catch the buses
Pedestrians
Mourners at Arthur's funeral
Public in the Courtroom.

The copyright of the novel *Cry, the Beloved Country* belongs to the Late Alan Paton Trust, 1947, 1976.

Dramatisation rights, including professional/amateur stage, television and video/sound recording, for *Cry, the Beloved Country* and *Lost in the Stars* are held by Kurt Weill and Maxwell Anderson and are strictly reserved. All enquiries should be addressed to Robert A. Freedman Dramatic Agency, Inc. at 1501 Broadway, Suite 2310, New York, New York 10036.

For performance rights of this adaptation contact Sargeant & Associates Literary Agency, PO Box 39310, Capricorn Square, South Africa 7948 or email roys@artscape.co.za.

ACT 1

SCENE 1

The setting shows a road; there is a street lamp at the top that could be mistaken for a gallows; to either side two distinctive acting areas. To stage left, a sense of interior. A rough-hewn wall backs this area. To stage right, rocks. Downstage of the set, soil. Bleak.

A Contemporary Schoolboy [Actor 13] *is discovering the novel for the first time. A Walkman identifies that he is from the 21st century. He carries a battered copy of the novel and a CD recording too. He slips the CD into the Walkman and turns it on. He listens as* ***Actor 12*** *enters.*

Recorded voice of Alan Paton There is a lovely road that runs from Ixopo into the hills. These hills are grass-covered and rolling and they are lovely beyond any singing of it. The road climbs seven miles into them to Carisbrooke; and from there, if there is no mist, you look down on one of the fairest valleys of Africa. About you there is grass and bracken and you may hear the forlorn crying of the titihoya, one of the birds of the veld.

The cry of the titihoya.

Actor 12		Below you is the valley of the Umzimkulu, on its journey from the Drakensberg to the sea; and beyond and behind the river, great hill after great hill; and beyond that and behind them, the mountains of Ingeli and East Griqualand.
Contemporary Schoolboy		Natal?
Actor 12		Natal, the beautiful place. The grass is rich and matted, you cannot see the soil. Stand unshod upon it, for the ground is holy being as it came from the Creator. Keep it, guard it, care for it, for it keeps men, guards men, cares for men. Destroy it and man is destroyed.
		*Like ghosts returning from 1946, the other characters emerge, startling the **Contemporary Schoolboy**. They each carry a suitcase.*
Actor 6		But the rich green hills break down. They fall to the valley below, and falling change their nature.
Actor 11		For they grow red and bare; they cannot hold the rain and mist, and the streams are dry in the kloofs.
Actor 4		Too many cattle feed upon the grass, and too many fires have burned it.
Actor 5		It is not kept, or guarded, or cared for, it no longer keeps men, guards men, cares for men. The titihoya does not cry here any more.
Actor 8		The great red hills stand desolate, and the earth is torn away like flesh. Down in the valleys women scratch the soil that is left, and the maize hardly reaches the height of a man.
Actor 10		They are valleys of old men and old women, of mothers and children.
Actor 9		The men are away, the young men and the girls are away. The soil cannot keep them any more.
Actor 3		And so, all roads lead to Johannesburg, whether you are white or black they lead to . . .

ACT 1 SCENE 1

All	Johannesburg!
Actor 3	If the crops fail, there is work in ...
All	Johannesburg!
Actor 3	If there is tax to be paid, there is work in ...
All	Johannesburg!
Actor 3	If the farm is too small to be divided fairly, some must go to ...
All	Johannesburg!
Actor 3	Where?
All	Johannesburg!
Actor 3	Where?
All	Johannesburg!
Actor 3	Johannesburg!

The sound of a Zulu hymn for safety on a journey. Train conductor's whistle.

SCENE 2

A railway station, Ixopo. **Commuters with suitcases.** *Rev. Stephen Kumalo [Actor 1] is there, with his suitcase. His black clothes are green with age, and his collar brown with age and dirt.*

***Actor 4** and **Actor 2** set up a rhythm, beating the earth with their feet in the Zulu manner. Train rattling on the tracks. It is travelling now.*

SCENE 3

On the train. **Stephen** *is there. All the passengers sit on their suitcases as seats.*

Actor 12		All roads lead to Johannesburg. The train climbs up into the green rolling hills of Lufafa ...
Actors Severally		Eastwolds ... Donnybrook ... to the great Valley of Umkomaas ... Hemu-hemu ... Elandskop ... down the Valley of Umsundusi ... Edendale ... Maritzburg ... Hilton ... Lion's River ... Balgowan ... Rosetta ... Mooi River ...
Actor 12		Thundering through the night, over battlefields of long ago on its way from Natal to the Transvaal ...

Actor 12 leaves the stage quietly. **Contemporary Schoolboy** *looks on, intrigued.*

Stephen is reading a letter.

Passenger [Actor 2] *[Addressing Stephen]* Mfundisi, what brings you out of Ndotsheni? Is it the business of the church? *[Stephen ignores him.]* Aaaaah, is it the business of the letter? *[Stephen drops the letter away from him.]*

Rev. Theophilus Msimangu *[Actor 4] emerges from the shadows into light as* **Stephen** *returns to the letter.*

Theophilus To the Rev. Stephen Kumalo, St Mark's Church, Ndotsheni, Natal, from The Mission House, Sophiatown, Johannesburg, September 25, 1946.

My dear brother in Christ:
I have met a young man here in Johannesburg. The young man's name is Absalom Kumalo and I understand he is your son. This young man is very sick and therefore I ask you to come quickly to Johannesburg. *[Theophilus touches Stephen's shoulder lightly.]* Come to the address above and there I shall give you some advice. I am, dear brother, Yours faithfully ...

Theophilus & Stephen 'Rev. Theophilus Msimangu' ...

***Theophilus** moves away.* **Stephen** *looks at his* **Wife** *as the train fades away and ceases its action.*

SCENE 4

Stephen's house, Ndotsheni.

Stephen	Mama ...
Wife	Baba?

*Stephen's **Wife** is cleaning a plate.*

Stephen	This is not an easy letter.
Wife	No, baba. What will you do then, baba?
Stephen	About what, my wife?
Wife	Baba, about this letter?
Stephen	Bring me the St Chad's money.

Putting plate and dishcloth down, she fetches the cocoa tin, and hands it to him. He studies it.

Wife	It must be done, Stephen.
Stephen	How can I use it? This money was to send Absalom to St Chad's.
Wife	Stephen, our son will never go now to St Chad's.
Stephen	How can you say that?
Wife	Baba, when people go to Johannesburg they do not come back.
Stephen	Oh, you have said it now. Now it is said. You have opened the door and because you have opened the door we have to go through. Only uNkulunkulu knows where we shall go.
Wife	Stephen, it is not I who opened it. It has been a long time open. But you would not see it, baba.

Stephen		We had a son. Zulus have many children. But we had only one son. And now as you say, when people go to Johannesburg, they do not come back. All those who have gone away, they do not write anymore, they do not go to St Chad's to learn the knowledge without which no black man can live. They go to Johannesburg and there they are lost. This money, this money . . . in my hands . . .
Wife		Baba, you are hurting yourself.
Stephen		*[Angrily]* Hurting myself?
Wife		Yes.
Stephen		I do not hurt myself, it is they who are hurting me. My own son, my own nephew, my own brother. They go away and they do not write any more. Perhaps to them it does not seem that we suffer. Go – go up and ask the white man at the store. Perhaps there are letters. Perhaps they have fallen under the counter, or been hidden amongst the food. Or the wind has blown them up the trees . . .
Wife		*[Crying out]* Stop it, Stephen. You are hurting me also.
		Pause.
Stephen		No. No. That I may not do.
Wife		Baba, you must go. Please, baba. Uhambe kahle, baba. *['Go well, Father'.]*
		She goes, re-joining the train as one of the passengers.

● ●

SCENE 5

On the train. **Stephen** *holds the St Chad's money.*

Passenger *[Referring to the money **Stephen** is holding.]* Hhayi, imali engaka, mfundisi. *['Hey, so much money!']* Hhayi, hhayi, put

	that away, mfundisi. *[He turns away from Stephen and addresses the young girl in the train.]* Heyi, ntombana, kanti awushelwe na? *['Hey, girl, have you received a proposal?']*
	*Receiving no encouragement from the **Girl**, **Passenger** turns back to **Stephen**.*
Stephen	My friend.
Passenger	I have a favour to ask. I return to the mines and there is little time to do these things. You know Sibeko?
Stephen	Yes.
Passenger	Well, Sibeko's daughter worked for a white man uSmith in Ndotsheni. When uSmith left for Springs, Sibeko's daughter went with them to work. And, Sibeko has heard no word of his daughter this twelve months.
Stephen	Awu, awu, awu, awu, awu.
Passenger	Here's the address, umfundisi. Please, I ask you to inquire.
	***Stephen** takes the dirty, thumbed paper.*
Stephen	Springs?
Passenger	Yebo, mfundisi. *['Yes, sir'.]*
Stephen	It is near Johannesburg?
Passenger	*[Nodding]* Angazi–ke lapho, mfundisi. *['I don't know'.]*
Stephen	I shall do what I can.
	***Stephen** takes out his purse and carefully stores the piece of paper in it. Then he is startled by what he sees out of the window.*
Stephen	Are those the mines, those white flat hills?
Passenger	That is the rock out of the mines, mfundisi. The gold has already been taken out of it

Stephen	Awu. How does the rock come out?
Passenger	Awu, mfundisi, we go down and then dig it out. Down in a cage, down a chimney so long that I cannot say.
Stephen	How does it come up?
Passenger	It is wound up by a great wheel, mfundisi. Wait, and I shall show you one.
	Stephen is silent. Then:
	There is the wheel, mfundisi. There.
All Passengers	Kwateba! *[Colloquially: 'The Mines']*
Stephen	Is that Johannesburg?
	Laughter as the train grinds to a halt.

All	Johannesburg!
	*Passengers disperse in all directions, leaving **Stephen** alone.*
Stephen	*[To himself]* Nkulunkulu, watch over me.

SCENE 6

In the city of Johannesburg. Township jazz. Bustle and noise of a busy city.

Newspaper Seller [Actor 2] Rand Daily Mail, Rand Daily Mail . . . read all about it . . . *[ad lib]* . . .

A Young Man [Actor 3] sidles up to Stephen.

Young Man UngumXhosa, mfundisi? *['Are you Xhosa, sir?']*

Stephen I do not understand.

Young Man You are Xhosa, then, mfundisi?

Stephen Zulu. From Natal, Rev. Stephen Kumalo from Ndotsheni.

Young Man Natal, bab' umfundisi? And so where do you want to go here in Johannesburg, mfundisi?

Stephen To Sophiatown.

Young Man Sophiatown, mfundisi? I know that place, mfundisi. Let me take you there, mfundisi. Come, mfundisi, I will take you there.

Newspaper Seller Rand Daily Mail . . . *[etc.]* . . .

They reach the bus queue.

Young Man Awu, mfundisi. This is the place of the buses. You must stand in line, mfundisi. Have you your money for the ticket?

Stephen Yes.

Stephen puts down his suitcase and eagerly takes out his purse and takes out a pound.

Young Man I shall get your ticket for you, mfundisi? Then you need not

SCENE 6

lose your place in the line. *[**Stephen** gives him the pound note.]* I am coming now with the ticket, mfundisi.

Stephen Thank you.

*The **Young Man** takes the pound and disappears.*

Newspaper Seller Rand Daily Mail ... *[etc.]* ...

*Waiting in line, **Stephen** grows fearful. The line moves forward, and again forward, soon he must enter the bus, and still no ticket. He leaves the line and walks to the corner, but there is no sign of the young man. He turns to someone in the line.*

Stephen Excuse me ...

*He is ignored. He approaches **Mr Mafolo** [Actor 6].*

Stephen Excuse me, brother. Where is the ticket office?

Mafolo What ticket office, Father?

Stephen For the ticket for the bus.

Mafolo You get your ticket on the bus.

Stephen Awu, awu, awu, awu.

Mafolo There is no ticket office.

Stephen I gave a pound to a young man, and he told me he would get my ticket at the ticket office.

Mafolo You have been cheated, my friend. Can you see the young man? No, you will not see him again. Look, come with me. Where are you are going?

Stephen The Mission House, Sophiatown.

They disappear amongst the crowds.

Actor 8	In due time they take their places in the bus. And it in its turn swings out into the confusion of the streets. Street after street, light after light, as though they will never end, at times at such speed that the bus sways from side to side, and the engine roars in their ears.
Newspaper Seller	Couple beaten and robbed in lonely house. Read all about it. Read all about it.
	[To the audience] In Sophiatown they alight at a small street, and there are still thousands of people about. They walk a great distance, through streets crowded with people. At last they come to a lighted place, the Mission House.
All	Sophiatown!
	Light change.

. . . .

SCENE 7

The mission house, Sophiatown. **Theophilus** *greets* **Stephen** *and Mr Mafolo outside.*

Theophilus	Mafolo.
Mafolo	. . . Mfundisi Msimangu, I bring a friend to you. Reverend Kumalo from Ndotsheni . . .
Theophilus	Siyabonga. *['Thank you']*.
Mafolo	Nisale kahle, bafundisi.
Stephen	Siyabonga, mfowethu *['Thank you, my brother']*.
Theophilus	Mfundisi Kumalo, I am glad to greet you. Please come inside. Is this your first time to Johannesburg?
Stephen	*[Nodding]* And I am much confused. I owe much to our good friend *[Indicating **Mafolo** who has left]* . . .

ACT 1 · SCENE 7

Theophilus	You fell into good hands. Mr Mafolo is a good son of the church. *[As they enter the Mission House.]* You must no doubt be tired and hungry after such a long journey.
Stephen	Yes. But I fear it is only the beginning.
Theophilus	Awu, awu.

***Father Vincent** [Actor 10] and **Father Lawrence** [Actor 11] are there.*

Theophilus	Father Vincent, Stephen Kumalo.
Vincent	*[Shaking hands with **Stephen**]* Ah, yes, Reverend Kumalo.
Theophilus	Father Lawrence.
Lawrence	Father ...
Stephen	*[As they shake hands]* Father.

***Theophilus** hands **Stephen's** suitcase to **Father Lawrence** who stores it.*

Vincent	*[Indicating that **Stephen** should sit]* Please ... Tell us of the beauties of Ndotsheni, brother.
Stephen	Beauties? It is only beautiful high up in the hills. Down in the valley it is a place of old men and women, mothers and children. When our young people go away many never return, many never write any more.
Lawrence	Yes, then the young men and the young girls, they come here to Johannesburg where they forget their customs.
Theophilus	They live loose and idle here. They become bored, so they turn to crime.
Vincent	You will learn much here in Johannesburg. It is not only in your place that there is destruction.

Theophilus	This is true, Father Vincent. *[He shows them a newspaper and reads out the headline.]* 'COUPLE ROBBED AND BEATEN, FOUR NATIVES ARRESTED.'
Vincent	Is it really necessary for them to say the word 'native' in such a headline? The fear only goes stronger. And white Johannesburg is already afraid of this black crime.
Lawrence	Enough crime talk for me tonight. Good night, gentlemen.

They say their goodnights as he leaves. There is a moment of silence.

Stephen	You will pardon me if I am hasty. But now I am anxious to hear about my son. Is he very sick?
Theophilus	I am sure you are anxious. You must think we are very thoughtless. Mfundisi Kumalo, your son is very sick. But it is not that kind of sickness. *[He nods at* **Father Vincent**.*]*
Vincent	It is another, a worse kind of sickness. I am chaplain at the Diepkloof Reformatory. Absalom has been in the reformatory.

***Stephen** is shocked.*

Stephen	The cause?
Vincent	Theft.
Stephen	A thief? Absalom … ?
Theophilus	He did very well at the reformatory. He became one of our senior boys. We had great hopes for his future, so he was released six months ago.
Theophilus	But we are now given to understand that Absalom again keeps the company of his cousin, Matthew. Father Vincent knows of this cousin and believes he can be no good for your son. We must find him.
Stephen	I see, I see. The father of Matthew, my brother, he lives here in Johannesburg too. John Kumalo, he is a carpenter.

Theophilus		*[With a smile]* He is one of our great politicians.
Stephen		A politician? John?
Theophilus		I hope I shall not hurt you further, but your brother has no use for the Church any more. He says that what God has not done for South Africa, man must do. That is what he says.
Stephen		This is a sorrowful journey.
Theophilus		I can believe it.
Stephen		What will the bishop say when he hears this?
Vincent		What can a bishop say? Something is happening here that no bishop can stop.
Stephen		How can you say so? How can you say it cannot be stopped?
Theophilus		*[Gravely]* It must go on, Stephen. You cannot stop the world from going on. My friend, *[Sitting alongside him]* I am a Christian. It is not in my heart to hate the white man. You will pardon me if I speak frankly to you. The tragedy is not the things that are broken. But the tragedy is that they are not mended again. Not only in Ndotsheni, even here in Johannesburg, the white man has broken the tribe. But again … *[With a look to Father Vincent, who disclaims the honour]* … there are some white men who give their lives to build up what is broken. But overall, it is fear that rules this land. *[__Father Vincent__ places a hand on __Theophilus's__ shoulder, suggesting he should stop now. __Theophilus__ laughs apologetically.]* These things are too many to talk about now. Come, brother, I have a place for you to sleep.

__Vincent__ leaves, bidding them goodnight.

Light change. __Theophilus__ lights a candle and hands it to __Stephen__.

Theophilus	This room is small but clean.
Stephen	I am sure it is.

Theophilus	Good night, brother. Shall I see you in the church tomorrow at seven?
Stephen	Of course.
Theophilus	Sleep well, my brother. You will need your strength. Good night.
	Theophilus leaves. Light change.
Actor 2	He stands for a moment in the room. Forty-eight hours ago he and his wife had been packing his bag in far away Ndotsheni. Twenty-four hours ago the train had been thundering through the unseen country. And now outside this little room, the stir and movement of people, but behind them, through them, one can hear the roar of a great city. Johannesburg. Johannesburg.
Stephen	Who could believe it?
	Fadeout.

• •

SCENE 8

Mission house, morning.

Theophilus	Good morning, my brother. This day begins the search for your son. Are you ready? *[Stephen nods.]* Come, let us go.

• •

SCENE 9

Zulu hymn as the two men walk along the road.

Actor 2	They walk up the street, and down another, and up yet another. It is true what they say, that in Johannesburg you can go up one street and down another till the end of your days, and never walk the same street twice.

SCENE 10

John Kumalo's carpentry shop. Two benches set. **John Kumalo** *[Actor 6] sits with his hands on his knees like a chief, talking to* **Actor 2**. **Stephen** *and* **Theophilus** *stand, a little intimidated, at a slight distance.*

Dubula [Actor 2] *[Talking to* **John Kumalo**] Uyabona–ke lestrike kumele sisimele. *['You see, this strike, we must take a stand'.]*

Stephen Good morning, my brother.

John *[Not quite able to make out the person greeting him]* Good morning, sir.

Stephen Good morning, John, my own brother, son of our mother.

John rises, smiling heartily.

John My own brother. Well, well, who can believe! What are you doing here in Johannesburg?

Stephen I come to find Absalom.

It seems that John wants to avoid this subject.

John *[Calling offstage]* Tea ... bring us tea ... for three people!

Stephen Is your wife Esther well, my brother?

John *[Smiling in a jolly and knowing way]* My wife, Esther, left me ten years ago, my brother.

Stephen And have you married again?

John Well, not what the Church calls married. But she is a good woman.

Stephen You wrote nothing of this, John.

John	Now, brother, how could I write? You people in Ndotsheni do not understand how life is here in Johannesburg. So, I thought it better not to write.
Stephen	Is that why you stopped writing?
John	That could be why I stopped.
Stephen	*[Sitting]* I do not understand. How is life different here in Johannesburg?
John	That is difficult, brother. You see I have had an experience here in Johannesburg. Johannesburg is not like Ndotsheni. One has to live here to understand it.

John begins to walk about the room. He speaks in a strange voice.

Down in Ndotsheni I am nobody, even as you are nobody, my brother. I am subject to a chief, who is an ignorant man. I must salute him and bow to him, but he is an uneducated man. Here in Johannesburg I am a man of some importance.

He begins to sway to and fro, not speaking to them, but to people who are not there.

I do not say we are free here. I do not say we are free as men should be. But at least I am free of the chief. He is a trick, my brother, a trick to hold together something that the white man desires to hold together.

He smiles in a cunning and knowing way, and addresses his visitors now.

But it is not being held together. It is breaking apart your tribal society. It is here in Johannesburg that the new society is being built.

He suddenly roars at his imaginary audience.

There is money here, gold, lots and lots of gold. It is the gold that builds the high buildings, the wonderful City Hall, the beautiful houses of Parkwood, all that is built with gold from the mines. But in fact it is not built on the mines. It is built on our backs, on our sweat, on our labour. What does a chief know about that? But here in Johannesburg we know.

A crowd roars its approval of John's rhetoric.

We know.

He sits down suddenly, takes out a large handkerchief and wipes his face. His **'Wife'** *[**Actor 8**] enters with the tea tray. There are no introductions. She stands aside.*

That is my experience, my brother. It is also why I do not go to the Church.

Stephen That, and your wife, Esther?

John Yes, both perhaps. You see, my brother, it is hard to explain. Our customs are different here.

Theophilus Are there any customs here?

John There is a new thing growing here, Father. Stronger than any church or chief. You will see it one day.

Theophilus And your wife? Why did she leave?

John *[With a knowing smile]* She did not understand my experience.

Theophilus *[Coldly]* You mean that she believed in fidelity.

John *[Suspiciously]* Fidelity?

Scared of the growing animosity, John's **'Wife'** *makes to go.*

Stephen Tea, tea, buyisa, mama. *['Tea, tea, bring it, mama'.] [Pointing to the* **'Wife'** *and deliberately interrupting the growing clash between* **Theophilus** *and* **John**.*]* Tea. That is very kind of you.

John's **'Wife'** *sets the tea tray down and leaves.* **Stephen** *pours.*

And now, my brother, I must ask you. Where is my son?

John is discomfited again at the mention of Absalom.

John	Well, you have heard no doubt that he is friendly with my son.
Stephen	Matthew? I have heard.
John	Well, you see, my brother, my son did not agree well with his second mother. So he said he would leave. He had good work so I did not stop him. Your son went with him.
Stephen	Where, my brother?
Theophilus	Last time I heard, he was, er, well, they were both working for a factory in Doornfontein. They stay with a Mrs Ndlela, here, at 105, End Street ...
Stephen	Can we not telephone this factory?
John	*[Laughing]* Telephone them? What for? To ask if they will give us his address? Or to ask them if they know Absalom Kumalo? Or to ask them if they will call him to the telephone? They do not do such things for black men here, my brother.
Stephen	Then we will have to go and see Mrs Ndlela.

The two priests prepare to leave.

John	It was more than a year ago, my brother. I do not know what you will find. You know how these young men are.

SCENE 11

The two priests begin walking once again. The Zulu hymn. Others join in.

Theophilus	My brother, I shall tell you one thing, many of the things your brother said are true. *[They stop walking.]* The white man has

the power, we too want power. But when a black man gets power, when he gets money, he is only a great man if he is not corrupted. Many of us think when we have power we shall revenge ourselves on the white man who has had power. Because our desire is corrupt, we too are corrupted, and the power has no heart in it.

Stephen Your words are wise.

Theophilus But I have only one great fear in my heart. That one day when they are turned to loving, they will find that we are turned to hating.

• •

SCENE 12

Mrs Ndlela's house. **Mrs Ndlela** *[Actor 8] a middle-aged, stout woman.*

Mrs Ndlela No, Absalom is not here. But wait. I had a letter … *[she dives into a suitcase of papers, rummaging]* … asking about the things they'd left behind. *[She finds the letter and looks up at **Stephen** for a moment, half curiously and half with pity, giving him the letter.]* There. His address – Mrs Mkize, 79, Twenty-Third Avenue …

Stephen *[looking at the letter, which he then hands back to **Mrs Ndlela**]* Alexandra.

Stephen *and* **Theophilus** *make to go.* **Theophilus** *steps back to* **Mrs Ndlela**, *leaving* **Stephen** *at a small distance.*

Theophilus Mrs Ndlela, why did you look at my friend with pity?

Mrs Ndlela *[Dropping her eyes, then raising them again]* He is an umfundisi.

Theophilus Yes.

Mrs Ndlela I did not like that Matthew. Nor did my husband. That is why he and Absalom left us.

Theophilus	I understand you. But was there anything worse than that?
Mrs Ndlela	I cannot say for I saw nothing wrong. But I did not like his cousin.
Theophilus	We thank you, Mrs Ndlela.
Mrs Ndlela	Uhambe kahle, mfundisi.
Theophilus	Usale kahle. *['Stay well'.]*

Mrs Ndlela picks up the walking hymn.

SCENE 13

The bus stop for Alexandra. ***Protestors*** *enter led by* ***Mr Dubula*** *[Actor 2] who approaches* ***Stephen*** *and* ***Theophilus***.

Dubula	AZIKHWELWA! *['We don't use these buses!']*
Crowd	AZIKHWELWA!
Dubula	I-AFRIKA!
Crowd	MAYIBUYE . . . *['Let Africa come!']*
Dubula	MAYIBUYE . . .
Crowd	I-AFRIKA.

Protest song begins. It continues throughout the scene.

Dubula	*[To* ***Theophilus****]* Are you going to Alexandra, mfundisi?
Theophilus	Yes, my friend.
Dubula	We are here to stop you, mfundisi. To persuade you if you use this bus, you are weakening the cause of the black people. We have determined not to use these buses until the fare is brought back again to fourpence.

Theophilus	*[Turning to **Stephen**]* I am very foolish, my friend, I had forgotten the boycott of the buses. I am sorry, brother.
Stephen	*[Humbly]* Our business is very urgent.
Dubula	*[Politely]* The boycott is also urgent. They want us to pay sixpence, that is one shilling a day. Six shillings a week, and some of us only get thirty-five or forty shillings a month.
Stephen	Is it far to walk?
Dubula	It is a long way, mfundisi. Eleven miles.
Stephen	Awu, awu, awu, awu. That is a long way, for an old man.
Dubula	Men as old as you are doing it, every day, mfundisi. And women, and some that are sick, and some crippled, and children. They start walking at four in the morning, and they do not get back until eight at night. They have a bite of food, and their eyes are hardly closed on the pillow before they must stand up again, and sometimes to start with nothing but hot water in their stomachs. I cannot stop you taking a bus, mfundisi, but this is a cause to fight for.
Stephen	I understand. We shall not use the bus.
Dubula	Thank you, mfundisi.
Theophilus	Siyabonga, mfowethu.
Dubula	Siyabonga.
Stephen	That man has a silver tongue. I am willing to walk.
Theophilus	*[Quietly]* That is the famous Dubula. A friend of your brother, John.
Dubula	From fourpence to sixpence to ten shillings, ayikona!
Protestors	Ayikona!

Thumbs are raised in the traditional gesture of defiance. **Stephen** *and* **Theophilus** *return the salute.*

●●

SCENE 14

The walking hymn begins again as **Stephen** *and* **Theophilus** *set off for Alexandra.*

Actor 9   So they walk many miles through the European city, up Twist Street to Clarendon Circle, and down Louis Botha towards Orange Grove. And the cars and lorries never cease, going one way or the other. After a long time a car stops.

The car is a toy, wire model as are made by young black South Africans and sold on the roadsides. **Contemporary Schoolboy** *becomes the engine driving the car. The driver is* **Arthur Jarvis** *[Actor 7].*

Arthur   Reverend Msimangu.

Theophilus   Yebo, nkosana *['Young Master']*.

Arthur   I thought it was you. Where are you going?

Theophilus   We are on our way to Alexandra.

Arthur   Ja, I thought you might be. Well, get in.

They do so.

Actor 9   This is a great help to them.

A Zulu folk song of thanksgiving begins.

As they drive, **Stephen** *smiles at having been helped in public by a white man; an unusual occurrence. At the turn-off to Alexandra they express their thanks.*

The song ends as the men tip their hats to each other. The priests alight.

Theophilus Siyabonga, nkosana.

Arthur Ngiyabonga, mfundisi.

Theophilus Siyabonga, nkosana.

Stephen Siyabonga.

Arthur Ngiyabonga, mfundisi. Go well, gentlemen.

Theophilus Nawe uhambe neNkosi. *['You go with the Lord too!']*

Arthur Bye-bye.

Actor 9 They stand for a while waiting for the man to go on, but he does not go on. He swings around, and is soon on the road back to Johannesburg.

*The car disappears but **Arthur** hovers onstage.*

Stephen Do you know that man?

Theophilus That man is Arthur Jarvis. He led a great fight against the petition to do away with Alexandra altogether. You see this place, my brother, it is not a happy place. As it is outside the boundaries of Johannesburg, we can buy land here. Own a house, sub-let rooms. But many of these rooms are now hideouts for thieves and robbers, even prostitution. These things are so bad that the white people from the surrounding suburbs wanted this whole place removed. But then this Jarvis he said …

Arthur *[Speaking to **Contemporary Schoolboy**]* The good things of Alexandra are more than the bad …

Theophilus He also said …

Arthur	Alexandra is a place where one can have something of one's own, a place to raise children in, a place to have a voice in …
Arthur and Theophilus together	… so that a man is something in the land where he was born.

Arthur exits. **Mrs Mkize** *[Actor 5] has appeared in her house.*

• •

SCENE 15

Mrs Mkize's house. The priests stand on the threshold.

Mrs Mkize	I do not know where Matthew has gone, mfundisi.
Stephen	When did he leave Alexandra?
Mrs Mkize	These many months. A year it must be, mfundisi.
Stephen	Had he a friend?
Mrs Mkize	Yes, another Kumalo, his cousin, Absalom. They lodged together.
Stephen	How did he behave himself, this young man, Absalom?

There is a pause. **Mrs Mkize** *is filled with fear.*

Mrs Mkize	I saw nothing wrong.
Theophilus	But you guessed there was something wrong.
Mrs Mkize	No, there was nothing wrong.
Theophilus	Then why are you afraid?
Mrs Mkize	I am not afraid.
Theophilus	Then why do you tremble?

Mrs Mkize	*[Sullenly, watchfully]* I am cold ... mfundisi.
Theophilus	Mrs Mkize, we thank you. Farewell.
Mrs Mkize	Go well, mfundisi.

They leave her. She stays. At a distance from her:

Stephen	There is something wrong.
Theophilus	I do not deny it. Brother, go up the hill, and you will find a place for refreshment and wait for me there.

Stephen *moves off, heavy-hearted, puzzled.* **Theophilus** *turns back to* **Mrs Mkize**'s *house and then he storms into it, slamming his prayer book down on a bench.*

Theophilus	Mrs Mkize, I am not from the police. I have nothing to do with the police. But there is an old man suffering because he cannot find his son.
Mrs Mkize	That is a bad thing, mfundisi.
Theophilus	It is a bad thing, Mrs Mkize. And I cannot leave you until you have told me what you would not tell him.

Mrs Mkize *sits down.*

Mrs Mkize	Mfundisi, it is hard for a woman who is alone.
Theophilus	It is hard for an old man seeking his lost son.
Mrs Mkize	I am afraid, mfundisi.
Theophilus	He is afraid also. Can you not see he is afraid?
Mrs Mkize	I could see it, mfundisi.

There is a long pause, then:

Theophilus	Mrs Mkize, what sort of life did they lead, this boy and his cousin?
Mrs Mkize	Mfundisi, they brought many things here, mfundisi, in the late hours of the night. There were clothes, and watches, and money, and food in bottles, mfundisi, and many other things.
Theophilus	Was there ever blood on them?
Mrs Mkize	No, mfundisi, I never saw blood on them.
Theophilus	So why did they leave?
Mrs Mkize	I do not know, mfundisi. But I think they were near to being discovered, mfundisi.
Theophilus	*[Picking up his prayer book]* Here, on this book you will swear you do not know where they are gone?

Mrs Mkize *reaches for it, her hand trembling, but is interrupted by* ***Theophilus***.

It does not matter now, Mrs Mkize. We thank you. Farewell.

He makes to go.

Mrs Mkize	Mfundisi!
Theophilus	Mrs Mkize?

Mrs Mkize		They were not near to being discovered. They were both discovered, mfundisi.
Theophilus		Yebo ...
Mrs Mkize		But uMatthew, mfundisi, he ran away. And the other one, Absalom, the police took him away. I heard that the magistrate sent him to the reformatory, mfundisi.
Theophilus		This I know. But he is no longer there. *[He waits for a moment for more intelligence. It is not forthcoming, so he demands:]* Where is Matthew?

Mrs Mkize remains silent.

Mrs Mkize, I understand your fear. We thank you. Stay well.

*As **Mrs Mkize** exits, **Theophilus** goes up to where **Stephen** is waiting.*

Theophilus	Our priest from England, Father Vincent, speaks well of this reformatory. He says that if any boy wishes to change, there is help for him there.
Stephen	But he is no longer there. This I am afraid of.
Theophilus	I, too, am afraid now.
Stephen	Yes. You became afraid when you sent me out of Mrs Mkize's house, and you went back to speak to her.
Theophilus	You are wise. I see that I cannot hide from you.
Stephen	It is not because I am wise. But because it is my son. What did the woman tell you about my son?
Theophilus	Come.

They exit.

SCENE 16

*A public hall. **Mr de Villiers** [Actor 11] appears in the auditorium. **Arthur** is on the stage addressing the meeting. Behind him two people hold a banner: NEW SOCIETY – MANKIND IS MARCHING.*

Mr de Villiers   It is a crying shame, ladies and gentlemen, that we should have to live with this crime.

Arthur   Mr de Villiers ...

Mr de Villiers   Listen to me. Don't we have the right to protect our own property?

Arthur   Mr de Villiers ...

Mr de Villiers   Must we live in fear, for the lives of our children? We need more police. It is the only answer.

Arthur   It is not the only answer. We will always have native crime to fear until the native people of this country are given worthy purposes to inspire them and worthy goals to work for.

Mr de Villiers   Oh, rubbish.

Arthur   It is only because they have neither purpose nor goals that they turn to drink and crime and prostitution. And not because it is their nature to do so. But because their simple system of order and tradition and convention has been destroyed by our civilisation. Now, I ask you, Mr de Villiers, which would you prefer, a law-abiding, industrious, purposeful native people, or a lawless, idle, purposeless native people? The truth is we do not know; we fear them both. And so long as we vacillate, so long we will pay for the dubious pleasure of not having to make up our minds. And the answer does not lie, except temporarily, in more police and more protection.

Mr de Villiers Mr Jarvis, do you seriously suggest that increased schooling facilities will lead to a decrease in juvenile delinquency amongst native children?

Arthur I am absolutely sure of it, sir.

Mr de Villiers I see, and now, who is to pay for this schooling?

Arthur We should pay for it. If we wait till native parents can afford it, we will pay more heavily in other ways.

Mr de Villiers Mr Jarvis, doesn't more schooling just mean cleverer criminals?

They disappear.

SCENE 17

The two priests on the road.

Theophilus Mfundisi Kumalo. There is something I have not yet told you that Father Vincent learnt at the reformatory. When Absalom left the reformatory, they made an exception in his case, partly because of his good behaviour, partly because of his age, but mainly because there was a girl who was pregnant by him.

Stephen Awu, awu.

Theophilus She came to see him there. He is fond of her and is anxious about the child that will be born.

Stephen Is he now married?

Theophilus No, he is not ...

Stephen Nkulunkulu ...

Theophilus But everything was arranged for the marriage. This girl lives in Shanty Town. It will not be difficult to find her there.

Shanty Dwellers *appear singing a Zulu hymn of hope. The* ***Girl****, visibly pregnant, is amongst them.*

Actor 3   All roads lead to Johannesburg. But the black people go to Alexandra or Sophiatown. And there they try to hire rooms or buy a share of a house. This night, this very night they are busy in Orlando. Many people are moving there because there is no other place to stay. Shanty Town!

As the other shanty dwellers move away the ***Girl*** *is left and the two priests approach her.*

Theophilus   Ntombazana *['Girl']*, we have come to inquire after Absalom. Umfundisi lo *['This']* is his father.

Girl   He went on Saturday to Springs and he has not yet returned.

Theophilus   *[Angrily]* Hhayi, suka, wena *['Rubbish']*, but this is Tuesday. Have you heard nothing from him?

Girl   Nothing.

Theophilus   When will he return from Springs?

Girl   I do not know.

Theophilus   *[Indifferently]* Will he ever return?

Girl   *[Hopelessly]* I do not know.

Stephen   *[Compassionately]* What will you do?

Girl   I do not know.

Theophilus   *[Bitterly]* Perhaps you will find another man.

Stephen *would like to interrupt and diffuse the bitterness, but before he can speak:*

Come, brother, you can do nothing here. Let us go.

Theophilus *takes* ***Stephen*** *off.*

Stephen   But my friend ...

Theophilus   My brother, I tell you, you can do nothing. I tell you there are thousands such in Johannesburg. And were your back as broad as heaven, your purse full of gold, and did your compassion reach from here to hell itself, there is nothing you can do.

*Slowly, silently the men withdraw, **Stephen** lagging, looking back at the isolated figure of the **Girl**. A Zulu hymn sung by the Shanty Town dwellers as they surround the **Girl** leading her upstage and away.*

*Suddenly **Stephen** stops walking, he looks upstage to the **Girl** and the group moving away. Then he turns to **Theophilus**.*

Stephen   But you do not understand. The child she is carrying is going to be my grandchild.

Theophilus   *[Angrily]* Even that you do not know. And if he were, how many such more have you? Shall we search them out, day after day, hour after hour? Will this searching never end?

***Stephen** reacts as though he has been hit, looking down.*

Stephen   Is that why you did not tell me about the girl?

***Theophilus** is silent.*

Let us walk. *[**Theophilus** does not move.]* Come.

Pause.

Theophilus   I am ashamed to walk with you. *[Long pause.]* Brother, I ask your forgiveness for my ugly words?

Stephen   You mean about the girl?

Theophilus   Yes.

Stephen   You are forgiven.

Theophilus   Sometimes I think I am not fit to be a priest.

Stephen	It does not matter . . .
Theophilus	I am a weak and selfish man.
Stephen	But God has put his hand upon you.
Theophilus	You are clever and you comfort me.
Stephen	There is one thing I have to ask you.
Theophilus	It is agreed.
Stephen	What is agreed?
Theophilus	That I should take you to see the girl again.
Stephen	It seems you are clever too.
	They laugh.
Theophilus	It is not good that only one should be clever. Come, brother.
Actor 10	And yet they are not really in the mood for jesting. They walk along the hot road to Shanty Town, and both fall silent, with many things in . . .

Actor 10 is interrupted; we move straight on to the next scene.

SCENE 18

*Arthur Jarvis in his study writing. The focus of the scene shifts to the front door of his home. Through the glass **two intruders** appear outside. Stealthily they try the door handle. It turns, the door swings open.*

Arthur Jarvis in his study.

The Intruders come into the hall of Arthur's house. One is carrying a Webley revolver, the other a lethal iron bar. They are wearing balaclavas. They are black. Eyes, shifting fearfully.

ACT 1 · SCENE 19

Arthur in his study.

*The **Intruders** standing against a wall. A **Houseboy** approaches carrying a tray set with tea things. The intruder with the iron bar strikes him to the ground. He falls. A crash of a tea tray being dropped, crockery falling and breaking.*

Arthur hears it in his study. He rises.

*The **Intruders** more fearful now.*

Staircase leading down into the hall. Arthur's feet as he comes downstairs, calling 'Hello' ...

The Intruders ...

Arthur's feet ...

The Intruders ...

Arthur's feet, 'Hello' again ...

Faces of the Intruders, the Webley is raised and fired.

Crimson image as the shot is fired. [End of DVD.]*

• •

SCENE 19

A street in the city.

Newspaper Seller
[Actor 6]   Read all about it. Read all about it. 'Well-known city engineer shot dead. Assailants thought to be natives'. Read all about it. Read all about it.

Father Vincent buys a paper.

---

*In the original South African production of the play the murder of Arthur Jarvis was recorded on video and played via a DVD projector onto the wall backing the interior space on the set.

Read all about it. 'Well-known city engineer shot dead. Murder in Parkwood'. Read all about it. Read all about it.

Father Vincent has entered the Mission House.

SCENE 20

Mission house. **Stephen, Theophilus** *and* **Father Lawrence** *are there. They each have a newspaper.*

Vincent This is a terrible loss for South Africa. Arthur Jarvis was a courageous young man, and a great fighter for justice. And it is a terrible loss for the Church too. One of the finest of all our laymen.

Theophilus He gave us a lift to Alexandra during the bus boycott.

Vincent *[To Stephen]* You might have known him too. It says he was the only child of Mr James Jarvis of High Place, Carisbrooke. That is in your part of the country, isn't it?

Stephen *[Sorrowfully]* Yes, I know the father. I mean by sight and name, but we have never spoken. His farm is up above

ACT 1 SCENE 20

	Ndotsheni. He sometimes rides past our church. But I did not know the son. Yet I remember, there was a small bright boy ... *[He stops]* ...
Actor 11	A silence falls upon them all. This is not the time to talk of hedges and fields, or the beauties of any country. Sadness and fear and hate, how they well up in the heart and mind, whenever one opens the pages *[he refers to the newspaper]* of these messengers of doom. Cry for the broken tribe, for the law and the custom that is gone. Aye, and cry aloud for the man who is dead, for the woman, his wife, and the child, his son.
	Actor 9 has appeared in a special light downstage centre. **Father Vincent** *leaves the room as does* **Father Lawrence**.
Actor 9	Cry, the beloved country, that these things are not yet at an end. The sun pours down on the earth, on the lovely land that man cannot enjoy for he knows only the fear of his heart.
Stephen	*[Rising]* I shall go to my room. Good night to you. *[He refers to the newspaper report.]* This thing. This thing. Here in my heart there is nothing but fear. Fear.
Theophilus	My brother, I understand. Yet it is foolish to fear that one thing in this great city, with its thousands and thousands of people.
Stephen	It is not a question of wisdom or foolishness. It is just fear.
Theophilus	Then come and pray, Stephen.
Stephen	I have no prayer left in me. I am dumb inside. I have no words at all.
Actor 9	Have no doubt, it is fear in the land. For what can man do when so many have become lawless? Who can enjoy the sun pouring down on the earth, and the lovely land, when there is fear in the heart? Who can walk quietly in the jacarandas when

their beauty is turned to danger? Who can lie peacefully in bed when the darkness holds some secret?

Father Vincent *has been isolated in light, stage left.*

Vincent | There are voices crying what must be done. A hundred thousand voices. But what does one do? One cries this, one cries another, and one cries something which is neither this nor that. Who knows how we will fashion a land where black outnumbers white so greatly? For we fear not only the loss of our possessions, but the loss of our whiteness. Some say crime is bad, but is it better to hold on to what we have and pay the price with fear? We do not know. We do not know. We shall live from day to day and put more locks on the door. Our lives will shrink and we shall live with fear.

Mr de Villiers *is isolated in light, downstage right.*

Mr De Villiers | It's a scandal, ladies and gentlemen, that we get so few police. This suburb pays more in taxes than most, and what do we get for it? A third-class police station. This is the second murder in two weeks. We must demand more protection. More police. Heavier sentences. We must have more police on the streets. It's the only answer.

Actor 9 | Cry, the beloved country, for the unborn child that is the inheritor of our fear. Let him not love the earth too deeply. Let him not laugh too gladly when the water runs through his fingers, nor stand too silent when the setting sun makes red the veld with fire. Let him not be too moved when the birds of his land are singing, nor give too much of his heart to mountain and valley. For fear will rob him of all if he gives too much.

The Girl *runs up to the Mission House calling desperately to the 'umfundisi'. The three downstage look at her briefly then merge away.* ***Theophilus*** *comes out and greets her.*

SCENE 21

Mission house.

Theophilus   Yebo, ntombazana?

Girl   Amaphoyisa have been to see me, mfundisi.

Theophilus   The police?

Girl   They were looking for Matthew and Absalom, mfundisi.

Stephen   What did you tell them?

Girl   I told them I had not seen him since Saturday, mfundisi.

Stephen   *[In torment]* And why did they want him?

Girl   *[Drawing back, frightened]* I do not know.

Stephen   *[Crying out]* And why did you not ask?

Girl   *[Tears filling her eyes]* I was afraid.

Theophilus   Did it seem heavy?

Girl   It seemed heavy, mfundisi. What is the trouble?

     Stephen *moves away from them.*

     What is the trouble?

Theophilus   Sizokutshela uma sesazi. Hamba. *['We'll tell you when we've heard. Leave!']*

     The **Girl** *moves off and* **Theophilus** *comes to* **Stephen**.

Theophilus   My brother, you are trembling.

Stephen   I am cold, very cold.

Theophilus	Let us go back inside. We shall have a fire and make you warm again.
	Stephen *and* ***Theophilus*** *settle into the Mission House during:*
Actor 6	Yet, it was true what Msimangu had said. Why fear the one thing in a great city where there were thousands upon thousands of people? His son had gone astray in the great city, where so many had gone astray before him, and where many others would go astray after him, until there was found some great secret that as yet no man had discovered. But that his son should kill a man, a white man!
	Stephen *is sitting, hunched over his stick.*
Theophilus	You have sat there too long, my brother. What have you found?
Stephen	Nothing.
Theophilus	Nothing?
Stephen	No, nothing. Only more fear and more pain. There is nothing in the world but fear and pain.
Theophilus	My brother . . .
Stephen	What is it?
Theophilus	Nothing.
Stephen	*[With passion and anger]* What breaks in a man when he can bring himself to kill another? What breaks when he can bring himself to thrust down the knife into the warm flesh, to bring down the axe on the living head, to cleave down between the seeing eyes, to shoot the gun that would drive death into a beating heart. *[He shudders.]* You are right, Msimangu. It is the not knowing that makes me fear this one thing, this thing in a great city where there are thousands upon thousands of people. But it is true I admitted it to

myself. The tribe is broken, and will be mended no more.
[He bows his head.]

Actor 8 It is as though a man borne upward into the air feels suddenly that the wings of miracle drop away from him, so that he looks down upon the earth, sick with fear and apprehension.

A Zulu hymn begins. **Stephen** *stands isolated and alone downstage centre.* **Theophilus** *steps towards* **Stephen,** *speaking directly to him.*

Theophilus I, the Lord, have called thee in righteousness.
I will hold thy hand.
I will keep thee.
And I will give thee for a covenant of the people.
To open their blind eyes, to bring the prisoners out of the
  prison and them that sit in darkness out of the prison house.

Two young men, wearing balaclavas, dash across stage.

I will bring light by a way that they know not.
I will make darkness light before them and Crooked things
  straight.
These things I will do unto them and not forsake them.
Dost thou not know that the everlasting God,
The Lord, the Creator of the ends of the earth
Faints not, nor is weary.

The same **two young men** *dash on again. They run up the road. At the top sudden light hits them from upstage. Police searchlights. They turn slowly. Slowly they remove their balaclavas. Then they turn upstage, clasping their hands together as if being handcuffed, and then move off.*

Theophilus *puts a hand out for* **Stephen,** *who enters the Mission House. The choir moves off.*

SCENE 22

*Mission house. **Theophilus** and **Stephen** are there when **Father Vincent** enters carrying a newspaper. He takes **Theophilus** aside and whispers to him. **Theophilus** is horrified.*

Theophilus [*Turning to **Stephen**]* My brother, what you feared is true.

Vincent Absalom has been arrested for murder.

***Stephen** falls onto a bench.*

Theophilus And his cousin Matthew has been arrested also.

A beat.

Vincent Would you like to go to the prison, Father? I have arranged it for you.

***Stephen** nods his head again and turns to take his hat.*

Stephen Yes. But I will go and see my brother first.

The three priests move off to John Kumalo's.

SCENE 23

*John's Carpentry Shop. **John** and his 'Wife' are there. Seeing his brother he turns to him.*

John And your business, brother, how does it progress? Have you found the prodigal?

Stephen He is found, my brother. But not as found in the Book. He is in prison, arrested for the murder of a white man.

***John** remembers that his son, Matthew, might have been with Absalom. Sweat forms on his brow. He wipes it.*

John	I am sorry, my brother.
	Stephen's silence is eloquent.
	You mean . . . ?
Stephen	Yes. Matthew, your son, was there that day.
John	Nkulunkulu! Nkulunkulu!
Stephen	There is a white priest at the Mission House. He is waiting to take me to the prison. Perhaps he will take you also.
John	Let me get my jacket and my hat, brother.
	His 'Wife' has got them for him.
	They go. John's 'Wife' exits.

· ·

SCENE 24

*The prison. **Stephen**, **John** and **Father Vincent** waiting. **Prison Warder** [Actor 7] brings **Absalom** on. Another **Prison Warder** indicates for **John** to join him and **Matthew**. **Vincent** and **Theophilus** look on.*

Stephen	My son.
Absalom	Yes, my father.
Stephen	At last I have found you.
Absalom	Yes, my father.
Stephen	And it is too late. *[Silence. Pressing him:]* Is it not too late? *[No response. **Stephen** sets his hat down.]* Answer me. Why did you do this terrible thing? *[No response.]* Answer me, Absalom. What . . . why did you carry the revolver?

Absalom	It was for safety, baba. This Johannesburg is a dangerous place. A man never knows when he'll be attacked, baba.
Stephen	Have they got it?
Absalom	Yes, my father.
Stephen	They have no doubt it was you?
Absalom	I told them. I told them I was frightened when the white man came. So I shot him. But I did not mean to kill him, baba.
Stephen	And Matthew?
Absalom	Yes, I told them. He came with me, but it was I who shot the white man.
Stephen	Tell me this, my child. You wrote nothing, sent no message for your mother and me. You went with bad companions. You stole and broke in and – yes, you did these things. But why?
Absalom	It was bad companions, baba.
Stephen	Was Matthew, your cousin to blame?
Absalom	Yes, he was.
Stephen	*[Furious]* Absalom, that is no answer, you must know that.

Vincent moves to join them.

Vincent	Do you wish to marry the girl at the Shanty Town?
Absalom	Yes, Father Vincent.
Vincent	I shall see what can be done.

John and Matthew have ended their interview. Vincent sees this. Matthew is led off.

Stephen, I think it is time for us to go.

Stephen	Stay well, my child.
Absalom	Go well, my father.

Prison Warder handcuffs *Absalom* and they move off. Suddenly *Absalom* stops and turns to *Father Vincent*.

Absalom	Father Vincent, do you have time to hear my confession?

Vincent looks at the *Prison Warder*, who indicates that he may. *Prison Warder* leads *Absalom* upstage, *Vincent* follows. *John* comes down to join *Stephen*.

John	*[Heartily]* Well, well, we must go at once and see a lawyer.
Stephen	A lawyer, my brother? For what should we spend such money? The story is plain, there cannot be any doubt about it.
John	What is the story?
Stephen	The story? These two young boys went to a house that they thought was empty. They struck down the servant. The white man heard the noise and he came to see. And then ... and then ... my son ... mine, not yours ... shot at him. He was afraid, he says.

John	Perhaps you do not need a lawyer. You see, my brother, if he shot the white man, there is perhaps nothing more to be said. But Matthew will need a lawyer. You see, brother, there is no proof that my son was there at all.
Stephen	What?
John	Yes.
Stephen	Not there at all?
John	Yes, yes.
Stephen	But my son . . .
John	Who will believe your son?

John walks away leaving Stephen flabbergasted.

Stephen	Nkulunkulu! Nkulunkulu!

The confession finished, Father Vincent comes up to Stephen.

Vincent	I think I can get a good lawyer to take the case. Absalom's defence will be that the shot was fired in fear and not to kill.
Stephen	You can understand that this has been a sorrowful journey. At first it was the search. I was anxious at first, but as the search went on, step by step, so did the anxiety turn to fear and this fear grew deeper and deeper, step by step.
Vincent	I understand that, my friend. But, Father . . . *[Stops.]* this is something . . . *[Stops.]* Really, this is something that . . . *[Stops.]* My friend . . .

Silence.

My friend, your anxiety has turned to fear, and your fear has turned to sorrow. But sorrow is better than fear. For fear impoverishes always, sorrow may enrich.

Stephen looks at him. His gaze is intense, hard to encounter.

Stephen		I do not know that I am enriched.
Vincent		Sorrow is better than fear. Fear is a journey, a terrible journey. Sorrow is, at least, an arriving.
Stephen		But where have I arrived?
Vincent		No one can comprehend the ways of God.
Stephen		It seems God has turned from me.
Vincent		That may seem to happen. But it does not, never, never does it happen. Your son's life can be changed. Because you are a priest this must matter to you above all else. More even than your suffering, or even your wife's suffering.
Stephen		That is true. Yet I cannot see how my son's life can be changed.
Vincent		Stephen, you are a Christian. You cannot doubt that. There was a thief upon the cross.
Stephen		*[Harshly]* My son was not a thief. There was a white man, a good man, devoted to his wife and child. And worst of all – devoted to our people. And now his wife, his child, they are bereaved because of my son. I cannot suppose it to be less than the greatest evil I have known.
Vincent		A man may repent.
Stephen		*[Bitterly]* Oh, he will repent. If I say to him, Do you repent? He will say ...
Absalom		It is as my father says. *[**Absalom** has moved out from the shadows. **Prison Warder** holds him.]*
Stephen		If I say to him, Was this not evil? ... he will say ... I
Absalom		It is evil.
Stephen		But if I speak otherwise, putting words in his mouth, if I say, What will you do now? ... he will say ...

Absalom	I do not know ...
Stephen	... or it is as my father says. *[His voice rising in anguish.]* He is a stranger. I cannot touch him, I cannot reach him. I see no shame in him, no pity for those he has hurt. Tears come out of his eyes, but it seems he weeps only for himself, not for his wickedness, but for his danger. *[He swings on **Absalom**.]* Speak what is in your mind. Speak the truth to me. Would you like a lawyer?
Absalom	They say one can be helped by a lawyer.
Stephen	It is true and Father Vincent knows of a good one. You told the police that Matthew was with you?
Absalom	I told them. And I have told them again.
Stephen	And then?
Absalom	And then Matthew was angry with me, and said that I was trying to bring him into trouble.
Stephen	Matthew was your friend?
Absalom	Yes, he was my friend.
Stephen	And now he will leave you to suffer alone?
Absalom	Now I see it.
Stephen	Till this, was he a friend you could trust?
Absalom	Yes, I could trust him.
Stephen	I see what you mean. You mean he was the kind of friend that a good man could choose, upright, hard-working, law-abiding?
Vincent	*[Quietly, to **Stephen**]* Old man, leave him alone. You lead him so far and then you spring upon him. He looks at you sullenly, soon he will not answer at all.
Stephen	*[Back to **Absalom**]* Tell me, was he such a friend?

No answer.

And now he leaves you alone?

Silence, then:

Absalom	I see it.
Stephen	Did you not see it before?
Absalom	*[Reluctantly]* I saw it, baba.

***Stephen** wants to ask why, in that case, he chose to continue, but **Absalom** is crying now. Compassion. A long pause.*

Stephen	Be of courage, my son. Do not forget there is a lawyer. Father Vincent arranged it.
Absalom	It is good, baba.
Stephen	And marry? Will you marry the girl?
Absalom	Yes, I can marry her.
Vincent	And be a father to your child.
Absalom	Yebo, baba.
Stephen	Father Vincent is going to speak to the Bishop to see if it can be done quickly. Then she will come and live with me in Sophiatown. And then we will go back to Ndotsheni and the child will be born there.
Absalom	It is good, my father.
Stephen	I have written to your mother. You may write to her too.
Absalom	I shall write, baba.

***Stephen** has taken a handkerchief from his pocket. He stuffs it into **Absalom's** pocket.*

Stephen	And wipe away those tears.
	Prison Warder leads *Absalom* away.
Vincent	You may thank God that we have got one of the greatest lawyers in South Africa.
Stephen	Forgive me, Father, but how do I thank God when I do not have the money to afford such a thing?
Vincent	He will take the case *pro deo*. Ah, yes, you have not heard of that before. It is Latin, and it means for God. So it will cost you nothing.
Stephen	He will take it for God?
Vincent	For God.
Stephen	For God? *[He weeps.]* For God! I have never met such kindness.
Vincent	The lawyer has told me to tell you that whatever happens Absalom will be severely punished. But if his defence is accepted, that he fired out of fear, it will not be the extreme punishment. While there is life there is hope, for the amendment of life.
	Stephen picks up his hat and they exit.
	The Contemporary Schoolboy watches as the lights fade down to a bench on which the *Schoolboy* sits. *Theophilus* comes over to him and sits down alongside him.
Theophilus	Who indeed knows the secret of the earthly pilgrimage? Who knows what keeps us living while all things break about us? *[He has taken the copy of the novel from the Schoolboy.]* Wise men write many books, in words too hard to understand. But this, the purpose of all our lives, the end of all our struggle is beyond all human wisdom.
	Fade to black.

ACT 2

SCENE 1

The road to Carisbrooke. **The Contemporary Schoolboy** *is there. An exquisite doll's house is set up on the top of the set.*

Actor 12 enters. He is carrying a hat.

Schoolboy   There is a lovely road that runs from Ixopo into the hills. These hills ...

Actor 12   No, no, no ... take it slowly.

Schoolboy   There is a lovely road that runs from Ixopo into the hills. These hills are grass-covered and rolling, and they are lovely beyond any singing of it. The road climbs seven miles into them, to Carisbrooke; and from there, if there is no mist, you look down on ...

Schoolboy & Actor 12   ... one of the fairest valleys of Africa.

Margaret [Actor 9] enters and sits down near the doll's house.

Actor 12   Up on the tops there is a house, and flat ploughed fields.

SCENE 2

The Farm High Place in Carisbrooke, Natal.

Actor 12   They will tell you it is one of the finest farms of this countryside. It is called High Place, the farm and dwelling-place ... *[He puts the hat on.]* ... of James Jarvis, Esquire, and it stands high above Ndotsheni, and the great valley of the Umkomaas.

The Police Captain [Actor 10] emerges up at the top and comes down the road to James, saluting Margaret as he passes her.

James Jarvis — The hot afternoon sun pours down on my fields. Rain, rain, there is no rain. *[He crouches to the earth.]* The plough rides uselessly over the soil. Hard as iron. Yes, Captain, but if I go up there to the tops, there I will find no sign of drought. The mists feed the grass up there. Even here, halfway up it was good. But now, year by year, the desolation eats back, mile by mile, from below, threatening High Place. Well, Captain, perhaps you have brought some rain for us?

Captain — I don't see any, Mr Jarvis.

James — Neither do I. What brings you out today?

Captain — Mr Jarvis, I have some bad news for you.

James — Bad news? Is it my son?

The Captain nods.

James — Is he dead?

Captain — *[Nodding again]* He was shot dead at ten-thirty this morning in Johannesburg.

James — Shot dead? By whom?

Captain — It is suspected by a native housebreaker. You know his wife and son were away. *[James nods.]* He stayed at home for the day, a slight indisposition. It appears that your son heard a noise and came down to investigate. The native shot him dead. There was no sign of any struggle.

James — *[Sitting on a stone]* My God!

Captain — I'm sorry, Mr Jarvis.

James — My God.

James tries to control himself.

Captain Mr Jarvis, I am instructed to offer you every assistance. There is an aeroplane waiting at Pietermaritzburg. You could be in Johannesburg by eight o'clock tonight.

James That is kind of you. What time is it?

Captain Half-past one, Mr Jarvis.

James Three hours ago.

Captain Yes, Mr Jarvis.

James Three hours ago he was alive.

Captain Yes, Mr Jarvis.

Margaret is watching the men intently now.

James My God! You didn't tell my wife?

Captain No, Mr Jarvis.

James She isn't strong. I don't know how she will stand it. Did they catch the native?

Captain Not yet, Mr Jarvis.

James moves forward towards the policeman, he stumbles and clutches the policeman's arm.

James Arthur was our only child, Captain.

Captain I think we should go, Mr Jarvis. Can you walk? I don't want to help you. Your wife's watching us.

James She's wondering, even at this distance, she knows something is wrong.

Captain It's quite likely. I tried not to show it, but ...

James   *[He stands up]* My God. There's still that to do.

*They go up the 'road', the **Captain** leaves. **James** approaches **Margaret**, who has risen.*

***James** takes a black veil and gently places it over **Margaret's** head and face.*

*She snatches it off. **James** takes it from her and places it back over her head and face. Again she snatches it off. **James** takes the veil once again. Then **Margaret** turns to him and slaps him across the face and collapses into his arms.*

He holds her. She is crying.

*Then **Margaret** takes the veil from **James** and puts it on. Then they turn to their coats and hats. **James** picks up both their suitcases. But, almost angrily, **Margaret** snatches her suitcase from him.*

*And as they move down the road towards the interior area stage left the **Schoolboy** has picked up a wire model of an aeroplane. We hear the roar of its engines. **Schoolboy** and model settle.*

• •

SCENE 3

*The Harrison home in Johannesburg. **James** and **Margaret Jarvis** and **John Harrison** [Actor 11] are there. **Harrison** takes their suitcases and sets them down.*

Margaret   How is my daughter-in-law, Mr Harrison?

Harrison   She's suffering from shock, Mrs Jarvis, but she's very brave. I brought them back here. I thought it best that they come here and not go back to the house.

Margaret   And my grandson, is he … ?

Harrison   He's taken it very badly. But that has given Carol something to occupy herself with. You're to go straight up. Top of the stairs, turn left, first bedroom on the right.

Margaret Let me go up first, James. *[He takes her hand, but she pulls away.]* I'll call you.

She leaves. There is a silence as the two men look at each other. To break it:

James Our daughter-in-law is strong. How fiercely she would defend Arthur when he and I would disagree about the native question and other political matters. I admired that.

Harrison Well, as you know, he was always speaking, here and there. You know the sort of thing. Native crime. More native schools. He kicked up a hell of a dust in the newspapers about the conditions of the compound system on the mines. He wanted the Chamber to ... *[He stops.]* ... Surely you'd like to talk about something else ...

James No, Harrison, you are doing me more good by talking.

Harrison Well, you know how it was. He and I did not often talk about these things. Not really my line of country. Tell the truth, these crimes upset me. We live in a state of fear in Johannesburg at the moment. I tell you we do not go to bed at night until we have barricaded the house. I asked Arthur about this once. He said we were to blame somehow.

James Arthur and I did not really see eye-to-eye on the native question, Harrison.

Harrison I must confess I did not always follow what he was saying. But he did have a kind of sincerity about him. I suppose if you had the time you could always understand what he was on about. He touched many people. *[He turns to a pile of papers.]* We saved all the telegrams for you. From the Archbishop, the Acting Prime Minister, the Mayor, and ... oh ... a native organization called the African Boys' Club, Gladiolus Street,

	which he started in Claremont. He was writing an essay when he ... at the end ... *[He picks up the essay from the table – there is only one page – and reads the title:]* 'A Private Essay on the Evolution of a South African'. I thought you might like to see ...
James	Yes, yes, I would like to see what he wrote. Arthur was clever. That came from his mother.
	Quietly, **James** *takes the essay from* **Harrison**. *He becomes engrossed.*
Harrison	Well, I'll ... I'll leave you to it.
	Harrison *moves into the shadows across stage right and sits.* **James** *sits down.* **Arthur** *has appeared alongside his father.*
James	21st September 1946.
Arthur	I was born on a farm, brought up by honourable parents. They were upright and kind and law-abiding. From them I learned all that a child should learn of honour, charity and generosity. But of South Africa I learned nothing at all.
	James, *hurt by this, stops reading. He puts the essay down and walks out of the room, disturbed.*
	Harrison *looks up at him.*
Harrison	Jarvis? You alright?
	James *does not respond. Eventually he makes the decision to return to the essay and take it on. He sits again, holding the essay.*
Arthur	It is not easy being born a South African. One can be born an Afrikaner, or an English-speaking South African, or a coloured man, or a Zulu. One can ride, as I rode when I was a boy, over green hills and into great valleys. One can see, as I saw when I was a boy, the reserves of the native people and see nothing of what is happening there at all. One can read the brochures

about lovely South Africa, land of sun and beauty sheltered from the storms of the world, and feel pride in it and love for it, and know absolutely nothing about it at all. It is only as one grows up that one learns that there are other things here. It is only as one grows up that one learns of the hatreds and fears of our country. And it is then, Dad, it is then that one's love grows deep and passionate, like a man may love a woman who is both true and false, cold and loving, cruel and afraid. And that's why I have devoted my life, that's why I have devoted my time, and my energy, and my talents to the service of South Africa. I no longer ask myself if this or that is expedient, but only if it is right. I don't do it because I am a Negrophile or a hater of my own, but because I can't find it in me to do anything else. It's ... it's the only way to end the conflict of my deepest soul. And in this I am fortunate ...

A crash of a tea tray being dropped, crockery falling and breaking.

Arthur *looks up.*

All the **Actors** *appear onstage now, except* **Actor 9**.

Actor 8 And there the manuscript and the page ended. This was the last thing that his son had done. When this was done his son had been alive. And then at this moment when he wrote ...

James 'In this I am fortunate ...'

James *puts the paper down.*

Actor 6 ... at those very words ...

Arthur 'In this I am fortunate ...'

Actor 2 ... at those very words that hung in the air, he had got up and gone down the stairs to his death.

Gunshot reverberates. **Actor 3** *is there, holding the revolver, pointed at* **Arthur**.

Actor 3	If one could have cried then …
Actor 8	… don't go down!
Actor 6	If one could have cried …
Actor 3	… stop, there is danger!
Actor 10	There was no one to cry.
Actor 11	'In this I am fortunate …'
Actor 2	And nothing more. Those fingers would not write any more.
Actor 11	'In this I am fortunate …'
Actor 3	Don't come down.
Arthur	… I hear a sound down below …
Actor 6	'In this I am fortunate …'
Actor 3	Stop, there is danger!
Arthur	… and I go to my death …
Actor 5	'In this I am fortunate …'

Arthur is standing alongside Actor 5 and, gently, she closes his eyes.

Arthur	… And I am not coming back any more.

Arthur steps down past Actor 3, pushing his hands and the revolver down as he passes. He exits. The others go, except Actor 8.

Margaret comes in.

Margaret	James.

He looks at her, startled.

James	How are they?

Margaret		Calm.
James		I will go up now.
Margaret		*[Referring to the essay* **James** *is still holding.]* What have you been doing?
James		Reading. *[He hands the essay to her. She holds it to her chest. He says quietly:]* Read it, it's worth reading.

He leaves.

Margaret catches her breath, forcing herself not to cry again.

Actor 8 So she sits down to read the essay. Finally she comes to the last words. 'In this I am fortunate', and she sits looking at them.

James returns.

And when he returns from upstairs, she looks at him, she is going to speak, he accepts that. Pain does not go away that quickly.

*He sits down next to **Margaret**.*

Margaret		*[Whispering]* It makes me proud.
James		I wish now that I'd known more of him. Like you did.
Margaret		It's easier for the mother, James.
James		You see the things he did, I've never had much to do with that sort of thing.
Margaret		His life was quite different from ours.
James		I am sorry I didn't understand it. *[In a whisper.]* I didn't know it would ever be so important to understand it.
Margaret		*[Embracing him]* My dear, my dear.

James		*[Whispering still]* There's one thing I don't understand, why it should have happened to him.

Boy trebles singing 'Kontakion for the Dead'.

● ●

SCENE 4

*Arthur's funeral. The family, **James**, **Margaret** (veiled), coats on, and for the first time we see Arthur Jarvis's son, a **Boy** (aged 14/15) [**Actor 13**], and Arthur's wife, **Carol** [**Actor 5**], heavily veiled. They are lined up, shaking hands with the mourners.*

Actor 2 The funeral was over. The brass doors opened soundlessly, and the coffin slid soundlessly into the furnace that would reduce it to ashes. And people that James did not know shook hands with him. It was the first time he had ever shaken hands with black people.

People singing Kontakion.

James, Carol, the Boy, and Harrison stay in position as Margaret moves into some separate light and the Russian hymn ends.

Margaret	The church was too small for all who wanted to come. White people, black people, coloured people, Indians – it was the first time James and I had sat in a church with people who were not white. The Bishop himself spoke, words that pained and uplifted. And the Bishop said too that men did not understand this riddle, why a young man so full of promise was cut off in his youth, why a woman was widowed and a child orphaned, why a country was bereft of one who might have served it, served it . . .

Choked with tears she turns away for a moment. James and Harrison turn to her, concerned. But then she stills herself and continues:

And the Bishop's voice rose when he spoke of South Africa, and he spoke in a language of beauty, and we listened, for a while, James and I, without pain, under the spell of the words. And pride welled up in my heart, pride in the boy who had been my son. Known to me, but a stranger to his father.

All exit except James and Harrison, who come downstage.

Harrison	Of course, Jarvis, you can stay as long as you like.
James	Thanks, Harrison. After the trial I'll stay to wind up Arthur's affairs.
Harrison	And what did the police say, if I may ask?
James	They're waiting for the houseboy to recover. They have hopes that he recognized the killer . . .

*the same **two young men** we saw in Act One dash on again. They run up the road. At the top sudden light hits them from upstage. Police searchlights. They turn slowly. Slowly they remove* *their balaclavas. As they do this **Jarvis** moves a step or two towards them. Then the young men turn upstage, clasping their hands together as if being handcuffed and they move off.*

***James** moves back to **Harrison**.*

James I hope to God they string them up!

Then he makes a gesture of apology.

Harrison I understand how you feel.

Harrison exits.

SCENE 5

*The courtroom. It is assembled around a bemused **James**. The public sit on the suitcases as benches.*

***Judge** [Actor 11]. **Absalom** and **Matthew** in the dock. **Clerk** [Actor 7], **Prosecutor** [Actor 10] to one side. **James**, on one side, **Stephen**, **Theophilus**, the **Girl**, **Black Public** on the other side.*

Clerk Silence in court!

Judge Matthew Kumalo, how do you plead?

Matthew Not guilty.

Judge Absalom Kumalo, how do you plead?

Absalom I plead guilty to killing, but I did not mean to kill.

Judge Why did you take the revolver with you?

Absalom Matthew said we must.

Judge And you did not say to Matthew, we must not take this revolver?

Absalom	No.
Judge	The Prosecution may proceed.
Prosecutor	After you left the deceased's house, Mr Jarvis's house, where did you go?
Absalom	I went into the plantation there at Parkwood.
Prosecutor	And what did you do there?
Absalom	I buried the revolver.
Prosecutor	Is this the revolver before the court?
	*The Clerk shows the revolver to **Absalom**.*
Absalom	Yes, it is the revolver.
Prosecutor	How was it found?
Absalom	I told the police where to find it.
Prosecutor	And what did you do next?
Absalom	I prayed.

Prosecutor	What did you pray then?
Absalom	I prayed for forgiveness.
Prosecutor	Did you pray for anything else?
Absalom	No. There was nothing else I wished to pray for.
Prosecutor	You made a statement before Andries Coetzee, Esquire, Additional Magistrate at Johannesburg. Is this the statement?

The Clerk shows it to Absalom.

Absalom	Yes, it is the statement.
Prosecutor	And every word is true?
Absalom	There is no lie in it, for I said to myself, I shall not lie any more ...
Prosecutor	In fact you repented?
Absalom	Yes, I repented.
Prosecutor	Because you were in trouble?
Absalom	Yes, because I was in trouble.
Prosecutor	Did you have any other reason for repenting?
Absalom	No, no, I had no other reason.
Judge	It is now two minutes to four. This court will adjourn until Thursday at nine a.m.
Prosecutor	As Your Lordship pleases.
Clerk	All rise!
Actor 5	In South Africa, men are proud of their judges, because they believe they are incorruptible. Even the black men have faith in

them, though they do not always have faith in the Law. In a land of fear, this incorruptibility is like a lamp set upon a stand, giving light to all that are in the house.

As the courtroom is broken down, **James** *passes across the path of* **Stephen** *who is shocked, recognizing* **James**.

Stephen, Theophilus *and the* **Girl** *to one side.*

Theophilus	My brother, you are trembling.

Stephen looks at him, but says nothing.

The Court will not hold the case again till Thursday. Tomorrow you must go out. Do something different. It will be good for you.

Stephen	There is one more thing I have to do before I go home. Is it far to Springs?
Theophilus	It is far. But I will take you. Come.

• •

SCENE 6

The Smith home in Springs. **James** *is there with* **Barbara** *[Actor 9].*

Barbara	Uncle James, I am so pleased you came to spend the night with us. It'll do you good to get away from ... Well ... it'll be good for you. I'm just popping out to the shop for some groceries. Won't be long.
James	Fine, Barbara. The garden is looking good.
Barbara	My pride and joy. But then the soil in Springs. Glorious. As it is all over the Reef.
James	Still, your aunt will be proud of you. She always said you 'could make a rose grow in the Kalahari'.

Barbara	Oh, how sweet of her. You make yourself at home, Uncle James, I won't be long.	

James takes a newspaper, walks downstage right, and sits.

Stephen appears at the back. He approaches through the garden.

Stephen	*[Tentatively]* Mr Smith … *[Louder now.]* … Mr Smith …

James lowers his newspaper and turns. Stephen is shocked.

James	Good afternoon, mfundisi …

Stephen has fallen.

Are you ill, mfundisi?

Stephen	I am sorry, mnumzana. I am sorry.

He tries to rise, manages and moves again, but falls again.

James	Are you ill, mfundisi?
Stephen	I shall recover, mnumzama.
James	Ufuna amanzi? *['Do you want water?']* Or is it food? Are you hungry?
Stephen	I am sorry, mnumzana.
James	What are you seeking?

Stephen, with trembling hands, pulls his purse out of his pocket. Papers fall out onto the ground. He stoops to pick up the old and dirty papers.

Stephen	I am sorry, mnumzana.

*He hands the piece of paper to **James**, who reads it.*

James	Yes, this is the place.

Stephen	I was asked to come here . . .
James	Yes.
Stephen	I was asked to come here, mnumzana. There is a man called uSibeko of Ndotsheni . . .
James	Ndotsheni, I know the place. I come from Ndotsheni.
Stephen	This man had a daughter who worked for a white man, Smith, of Ixopo –
James	Yes, yes.
Stephen	When Smith moved to Springs the daughter of Sibeko went also . . .
James	Yes.
Stephen	. . . to work for them.
James	Yes.
Stephen	Now Sibeko has not heard from his daughter these twelve months, and he asked – I am asked – to inquire about this girl.
James	Mfundisi, I am a visitor here and the mistress of the house is out shopping. But she will soon be returning, and you may wait for her if you wish.
	Stephen sits. Silence.
	I know you, mfundisi.
	Stephen averts his gaze.
	There is something between you and me, but I do not know what it is. You are in fear of me, but I do not know what it is. *[Approaching Stephen.]* You need not be in fear of me.
Stephen	It is true, mnumzama. You do not know what it is.

James	I do not know, but I desire to know.
Stephen	I doubt if I could tell it, mnumzama.
James	You must tell it, mfundisi. Is it heavy?
Stephen	It is very heavy, mnumzama. It is the heaviest thing of all my years.
James	Tell me; it will lighten you.
Stephen	I am afraid, mnumzama.
James	I can see that you are afraid, mfundisi. It is that which I do not understand. But I tell you, you need not be afraid. I shall not be angry. There will be no anger in me against you.
Stephen	This thing that is the heaviest thing of all my years, is the heaviest thing of all your years also.

*A moment of bewilderment for **James**. Then it comes to him.*

James	You can mean only one thing; you can mean only one thing. But still I do not understand.

***Stephen** looks up at **James**.*

Stephen	It was my son that killed your son.

*They are silent. **James** walks away from him. He looks out for a long while. Behind him **Stephen** picks up his stick and hat and begins to move off.*

***James** goes back to him.*

James	I have heard you, mfundisi. I understand what I did not understand. There is no anger in me.
Stephen	Mnumzama.

***Barbara** comes on. She sees **Stephen** and is irritated.*

Barbara	Uncle James?	
James	This native is looking for the daughter of a man called Sibeko. She used to work for you in Ixopo. They haven't heard from her in months.	
Barbara	Well, I had to send her away. She was good when she first started, but she turned bad. She started brewing liquor in her room. They arrested her and sent her to jail for a month ... well, I couldn't take her back after that, could I?	
James	You don't know where she is?	
Barbara	Of course I don't know. *[As she exits.]* I don't care.	
James	She does not know, mfundisi. You were shocked when you saw me. How did you know me?	
Stephen	I have seen you riding past Ndotsheni, past the church where I work.	
James	Perhaps you saw the boy also. He too used to ride past Ndotsheni. On a red horse with a white face. And he carried wooden guns, here in his belt, as small boys do.	
Stephen	Yes, I remember. There was a brightness in him.	
James	Yes, yes, there was a brightness in him.	
Stephen	Mnumzama, it is a hard word to say. But my heart holds deep sorrow for you, and for the inkosikazi, and for the young inkosikazi, and the boy.	
James	Yes. Go well, mfundisi.	
Stephen	Stay well, mnumzama.	

The two men watch each other as the courtroom is re-assembled around them. When it is set, they go to their respective places.

SCENE 7

The Courtroom.

Clerk   Silence in court! Defendants rise.

Judge   This Court has found you, Matthew Kumalo, not guilty of murder, and you are accordingly discharged. This Court has found you, Absalom Kumalo, guilty of the murder of Arthur Trevelyan Jarvis. I cannot find any extenuating circumstances. This Court has a solemn duty to protect society against the murderous attacks of dangerous men, whether they be old or young, and to show clearly that it will punish fitly such offenders. Have you anything to say before I pronounce sentence?

Absalom   I have only this to say. Yes, I killed this man, but I did not mean to kill him, only I was afraid.

Judge   I sentence you, Absalom Kumalo, to be returned to custody, and to be hanged by the neck until you are dead. And may the Lord have mercy on your soul.

A Zulu hymn of mourning.

*The **Judge** rises and leaves as do all the others. **Absalom** is led away by a **Prison Warder**.*

***John** and **Matthew** are downstage right, a sense of triumph. **Stephen** confronts them. The hymn continues in the background.*

Stephen	Matthew, leave us. I wish to speak to your father.
Matthew	Yebo, baba. *[Matthew exits.]*
Stephen	There is one last thing before I go home to Ndotsheni.
John	You are my older brother. Speak what you wish.
Stephen	Your politics, my brother. Where are they taking you?
John	My politics are my own.
Stephen	Do you hate the white man, brother?
John	I hate no man. I hate only injustice.
Stephen	Injustice? Injustice. I have heard that some of the things you say are dangerous. I have heard that they are watching you, that they will arrest you when it is time. I also hear it is the things said in your shop that they do not like.
John	In my shop? Who would know what is said in my shop?
Stephen	Do you know every man who comes into your shop? Could a man not be sent to your shop to deceive you? I have heard that a man might have been sent there to deceive you.
John	Who?
Stephen	A friend.
John	You heard that?
Stephen	*[Ashamed of the lie]* I heard it.

John	What friend would do this to me?
Stephen	My son has such a friend.
John	Your son? *[Then the meaning of it comes to him and he roars:]* You may not speak to me like that! You may not! We are no longer brothers!

John exits.

The hymn rises in power.

- - -

SCENE 8

The prison. **Stephen, Theophilus** *and the* **Girl** *are there.* **Absalom** *enters, led by the* **Prison Warder**. *He has a surge of hope and half runs to his father. He stands in front of him, trembling and shaking.*

Stephen	*[Realizing, speaking gently]* We are come for the marriage.

Absalom steps back; hope has died.

My son, here is your wife that is to be.

Absalom and the Girl take each other's hands, without life, holding loosely. Silence as they look at each other.

Absalom	Are you in health?
Girl	I am.
Stephen	Are you in health?
Absalom	I am.

***Father Vincent**, in his vestments, comes in.*

Vincent	Is everything ready?

SCENE 8

They all turn and move upstage.

Actor 10   Father Vincent reads to them from his book. Then he asks the boy if he takes this woman, and he asks the girl if she takes this man. And when they answer as is laid down in the book, for better for worse, for richer for poorer, in sickness and in health, till death do them part, he marries them and they sign.

*The hymn that has continued behind all this changes to one of celebration, swells for a moment and then goes to background once again and stops. The **Girl** kisses **Absalom** on the cheek. Then the **Girl**, **Theophilus** and **Father Vincent** go.*

Stephen   I am glad you are married.

Absalom   I am also glad, my father.

Stephen   I shall care for your child as if it were my own.

Absalom   When does my father return to Ndotsheni?

Stephen   Tomorrow.

Absalom   Tomorrow, baba?

Stephen   Yes, my son, tomorrow.

Absalom   Baba?

Stephen   Yes?

Absalom   Will you tell Mother that I remember her?

Stephen nods.

Baba ...

Stephen   Yes, my son.

Absalom   I have money in a Post Office Book. Nearly four pounds is

	saved. It is for the child, baba. They will give it to you at the office.
Stephen	I shall get it.
Absalom	Baba ...
Stephen	Yes, my son?
Absalom	When the child is born, if it is a son, baba, I should like his name to be Peter.
Stephen	Peter. And if it is a daughter?
Absalom	No, if it is a daughter, baba, I have not thought of any name, baba.
	*Short silence. Then **Absalom** drops onto his knees, sobbing.*
	Baba!
Stephen	Yes, my son?
Absalom	I am afraid, baba. Baba, I am afraid of the hanging, baba.
Stephen	Be of courage, my son.
Absalom	Please, baba ...
Stephen	Be of courage, my son ...
	*The **Prison Warder** comes to them and forces **Absalom**'s arms behind his back **Absalom** is taken off and **Stephen** leaves.*

• •

SCENE 9

	*Park Station, Johannesburg. Commuters. **James**, with his suitcase, is there with **Harrison**.*
James	I cannot thank you enough, Harrison.

Harrison		My love to Margaret, and to Carol and the boy. I'll come down and see you one of these days.
James		You'd be welcome, Harrison, very welcome.
Harrison		Oh, er, Jarvis, there is one thing I wanted to say, Jarvis. About the sentence. I know you can't bring the dead back, but it was right, absolutely right. It could have been no other way. Had it been any other way, I'd have felt there was no justice in the world.
James		Justice? Yes, I suppose so. But why did it have to be my son who needed this justice?
Harrison		*[After a beat]* There you have me, Jarvis.
James		Goodbye, Harrison, and thank you again.

They leave by different ways as **Stephen** *with his suitcase and the* **Girl**, *with a paper carrier, enter with* **Theophilus** *and* **Father Vincent**.

Theophilus	As for Absalom, it is the Governor-General-in-Council who must decide if there will be mercy.
Stephen	And if they decide against him?
Vincent	As soon as we hear, we will let you know.

The men shake hands.

Theophilus	Goodbye, my friend.
Stephen	Father Msimangu.
Theophilus	Mfowethu.
Stephen	You, friend of friends. Father Vincent ... *[**Father Vincent** unexpectedly embraces **Stephen**, who laughs gently.]* ... friend of friends.

The **Station Master's** *whistle blows.*

Theophilus	Nihambe kahle.
Stephen	Nisale kahle.

Theophilus and *Father Vincent* go.

The Boy runs a model, wire train down a track built into the 'road'.

Actor 11	The train steams and whistles its way over the Transvaal veld. At Volksrust it winds down the escarpment into the hills of Natal, thundering over battlefields of long ago. Mooi River, Balgowan, Lion's River to Pietermaritzburg, across the great valley of the Umsundusi, Elandskop, across the valley of the Umkomaas. Donnybrook, Eastwolds and Lufafa. And at Ixopo it runs beside the lovely road that goes into the hills.

SCENE 10

Ndotsheni. **Stephen** *with suitcase; the* **Girl** *with paper carrier;* **Stephen's Wife**. **Stephen** *embraces his* **wife**. *The* **Boy** *picks up his model train and greets* **James** *and they exit.*

Stephen	Mama.
Wife	Baba.

She embraces the **Girl** *as ululations and cries break out, greeting the returned* **Stephen**.

The three of them begin the walk to the Kumalo home, through the fields. Villagers cry out to them as they pass.

Actor 4	Awu, mfundisi, you are back!
Actor 3	Our mfundisi is back!
Actor 2	It is dry here, mfundisi.

Actor 6		There is no milk. Without milk there is no hope for the children, mfundisi.
Actor 3		The child of Kuluse is very sick.
Actor 4		The maize does not reach the height of man. We cry for rain, mfundisi.
Stephen		Where do we get water then?
Villager 4		The women must go to the river, mfundisi, that comes from the place of uJarvis.
Stephen		UJarvis?
Actor 4		Yes ...
Stephen		*[Taken aback at the mention of the name]* How is uJarvis?
Actor 4		UJarvis returned yesterday. But Unkosikazi Wakhe, his wife, returned some weeks ago, with the young wife and a small boy. I work there now, mfundisi.
Stephen		Awu, awu, awu.
Actor 4		We, mfundisi, angikutshele indaba ungayibuzanga. *['Let me tell you what you didn't ask.']*
Actor 4		It is known.
Stephen		It is known?
Actor 4		Yes, mfundisi, it is known.

Actor 4 goes off. Now a series of strange tremulous cries begins, called across the hills. Actor 4 arrives at the top with the 'doll's house' and sets it down.

Actor 3		You are returned, mfundisi.
Actor 6		We are satisfied, mfundisi.

Actor 7	We are hungry, mfundisi, feed us with your words.
Actor 3	Mfundisi, we give thanks for your return.
Actor 6	Mfundisi, you have been too long away.

James brings Margaret, still in mourning, on at the top and settles her. He goes to look out at the back.

• •

SCENE 11

St Mark's Church, Ndotsheni. **Stephen** *enters, and then kneels in prayer.*

Actor 7 enters.

Actor 7	Stephen begins to pray in his church. He prays for his son, for the forgiveness of his trespasses. He prays for the girl, that she may be welcome in Ndotsheni. He prays for her child to be, the grandchild he has promised to raise as his own child. But is this enough? It is not enough, so he prays for the restoration of Ndotsheni, but he knows that it is not enough either. Somewhere down here upon the earth, men must come together, do something, for there had never been such a drought in this country. And as he finishes his prayer, he realizes how far he has travelled since that journey to Johannesburg. The great city had opened his eyes to something that had begun and now must be continued.

Stephen has picked up a large book from under a bench and begins to look through it.

A small, white Boy [Actor 13] dashes into the church. He carries a riding crop. The Boy sees the priest and whips his cap off. Wife and Girl can be seen in the backroom, busy with things.

Boy	Good morning.

Stephen	Good morning, nkosana. It is a hot day for riding.
Boy	I don't find it hot. Is this your church?
Stephen	Yes, this is my church.
Boy	I go to a church school, St Mark's. It is the best school in Johannesburg. We've a chapel there.
Stephen	St Mark's. This church is St Mark's also.
Boy	I know, that's why I was keen to see it. Is that your house next door to the church?
Stephen	Yes. It is my house.
Boy	It is a nice house.
Stephen	A priest must always keep a nice house. You have seen some of our other houses, perhaps?
Boy	Oh yes, on the farm where I stay. But they're not so nice as your one. Is this your work over here?

He refers to a large book that is lying open.

Stephen	Yes, it is.
Boy	It looks like Arithmetic?
Stephen	Yes, it is Arithmetic. Those are the accounts of the church.
Boy	I didn't know that churches had accounts. I thought only shops had those.

Stephen laughs.

Why are you laughing?

Stephen	I am just laughing, nkosana.
Boy	Inkosana? That's little inkosi, isn't it?

Stephen	Yebo. 'Little master', it means.
Boy	Ngiyakuzwa. That means, 'I hear you', not so? *[Stephen nods.]* I would like to learn Zulu. Teach me some other words.
Stephen	*[Laughing]* I will gladly. Let's see ... Tree is umuthi. But medicine is also umuthi, because you see our medicines come mostly from trees.
Boy	Umuthi ...
Stephen	Isithuthuthu ...
Boy	Isi-thu-thu-thu ...
Stephen	Motorbike is isithuthuthu, from the sound that the motorbike makes.
Boy	*[With delight]* Isithuthuthu!
Stephen	Would you like a glass of water?
Boy	Can't we go to your house? I would like a drink of milk. Ice-cold, from the fridge.
Stephen	Nkosana, there are no fridges in Ndotsheni.
Boy	Well, just ordinary milk will do then, mfundisi.
Stephen	Nkosana, there is no milk in Ndotsheni.
Boy	I would like water then, mfundisi.
Stephen	Mama ...
Wife	Baba?
Stephen	Awungiphe amanzi. Unkosana womile. *['Mama, bring me water. Little master is thirsty.']*
Wife	Kulungile, baba. *['OK, Father.']*

Stephen		Are you staying here long?
Boy		Not very long. These are not real holidays now. We are here for special reasons. *[Stephen stares at him.]* Water is amanzi? *[Stephen does not answer.]* Mfundisi? Mfundisi?
Stephen		Yes, my child?
Boy		Water is amanzi, mfundisi?
Stephen		Yes, yes …

*Stephen's **Wife** comes into the church with the glass of water.*

Stephen		*[To the **Boy**]* This is my wife. Lo umzukulu kaJarvis. *['This is the grandson of Jarvis.']*
Wife		Hawu, baba, ngimangele. *['I am overcome.']* Angazi ukuthi ngithini. *['I do not know what to say.']*

*The **Boy** bows to her. She looks at him with sorrow.*

Boy		Ngiyakuzwa.

Wife takes a step back in fear.

Stephen		Yilo lodwa igama alaziyo. *['That is the only word he knows.']* *[**Wife** backs out of the church. **Stephen** turns to the **Boy** and claps his hands in astonishment.]* Awu! Awu! Soon you will be speaking better than many Zulus.
Boy		I think Zulu will be easy to learn. What's the time, mfundisi?
Stephen		Twelve o'clock.
Boy		Jeepers, creepers, it's time I was off. Thanks for the water. *[He steps out of the church onto the road. Then he turns back.]* Mfundisi, why is there no milk in Ndotsheni? Is it because the people are poor?
Stephen		Yes.

Boy	And what do the children do?
Stephen	They die, my child. Some are dying now.
Boy	Who is dying now?
Stephen	The small child of Kuluse.
Boy	Didn't the doctor come?
Stephen	Yes, he came.
Boy	And what did he say?
Stephen	He said the child must have milk.
Boy	And what did the parents say?
Stephen	They said, Doctor, we have heard what you say.
Boy	*[In a small voice]* I see. *[He raises his cap solemnly.]* Goodbye, mfundisi.

*He leaves and joins **James** up at the top, looking out. **Margaret** is still there.*

• •

SCENE 12

*Evening. **Stephen** and his **Wife**.*

*A **Villager** enters with **Kuluse**, who is carrying something.*

Actor 4	Baba mfundisi! Mama mfundisi!
Stephen	Yes?
Actor 4	I have a message for you from uJarvis.
Stephen	UJarvis?

	Actor 4	Yebo, mfundisi. Was the small white boy here today, mfundisi?
		***Stephen** reacts quickly, fearfully.*
	Stephen	Yebo.
	Actor 4	We were working in the trees when this small boy came riding up. He and his grandfather talked about the children of Ndotsheni. Uzobona ukuthi ngiphetheni. *['You'll see what I've got.']*
	Kuluse	Milk, milk … ubisi.
		***Kuluse** reveals what he is carrying: a milk can.*
		Milk, milk, mfundisi. For the small children, mfundisi, only those not yet at school.
		***Stephen** laughs with delight.*
		Every morning I shall come and take back the can when it is empty. This will be done until the drought breaks and we have milk again. Where shall we put the can?
	Wife	In the back, there is a room at the back of the church.
		***Kuluse** takes the can offstage.*
	Actor 4	Uzwile, Kuluse. *['You have heard, Kuluse.']* We bab' umfundisi … *['Hey, reverend …']* you would surely have a message for uJarvis?
		***Stephen** stutters and stammers, and at last points his hands up at the sky.*
		Ah, Nkulunkulu will bless him. Uyazi, mfundisi. *['You know, reverend …']* I have worked there only a week, but the day he says die, I shall die.
		*The **Villagers** go.*

Stephen	*[To his **Wife**]* Give me my jacket. I have to go and thank Jarvis myself.
Girl	Baba ... baba ... baba!
	*The **Girl** comes running on carrying two letters.*
Stephen	Yebo?
Girl	Baba, two letters from Johannesburg!
Wife	Johannesburg?
	Stephen *takes the letters. With fear he opens the first letter and reads.* ***Wife*** *and* ***Girl*** *watch tensely. After a moment:*
Stephen	What is the date today?
Wife	Monday the fifth, baba. It has come then, Stephen? *[He nods.]* Give it to me. *[He does so, she takes it and reads it]* It is not good to sit idle. Finish your other letter and then go and write your sermon.
Stephen	*[Opening the other letter.]* This is from ...
Wife	From him?
Stephen	Yes. From him.
	*His **Wife** takes the letter.*
	Absalom *appears amongst them. He sits opposite his father, who at a given moment looks up at him.*
Wife	My dear Mother and Father: I hope you are in health even as I am. They told me this morning that there would be no mercy for the thing that I have done. So I shall not see you or Ndotsheni again. There is no more news here, so I close my letter. But if I were back at Ndotsheni I would not leave it again. Give greetings to my wife.

ACT 2 SCENE 12

>   Your son,
>
>   Absalom . . .
>
> *Thunder rumbles.*
>
> *The women leave.* ***Stephen*** *sits in the lightning as the thunder grows louder and louder.* ***Margaret*** *and the* ***Boy*** *leave up at the top.*
>
> ***Villagers*** *scatter through the storm.*

• •

SCENE 13

> ***Stephen*** *in the church.* ***James*** *comes in, seeking shelter. He sits down. The two men listen to the storm. After a long time:*

James   It won't last much longer.

Stephen   The storm or the church?

> *They smile. There is a short silence. Sound of rain and thunder from outside.*

James   *[Without looking at **Stephen**]* Is there mercy?

> ***Stephen*** *shakes his head.*

Is there a date set?

Stephen   The fifteenth day. At dawn.

James   I understand.

Stephen   On the night of the fourteenth day I shall go to the place I have been to twice before. I shall go and keep vigil on the mountain.

James   When it comes to the fifteenth day, at dawn, I shall remember.

	[The storm abates. He listens. The thunder is farther away.] Do you hear that?
Stephen	What?
James	Do you hear the rushing of the streams?
Stephen	Indeed, dead streams come back to life.
James	Why, mfundisi, why should the streams ever have been dead in the first place?
Stephen	That, mnumzana, is a secret.
James	And pain and suffering?

Stephen is taken aback for a moment, then:

Stephen	These are secrets too. Love and kindness are secrets too. I have learned that love and kindness can pay for pain and suffering.
James	Can they?
Stephen	Let me remind you of your kindness for sending us the milk.

James makes a gesture of dismissal.

	No, mnumzana, the milk is not nothing. Though when it came I could say nothing. All I could do was point at the sky. But the milk is everything. A small child is alive today because of that milk.
James	That I did not know.

The two men stare at each other for a moment.

Stephen	The boy!

Stephen laughs gently, conceding.

	He is like him.
James	*[Laughing gently too]* He is, isn't he?

Stephen		There is a brightness in him.
James		As in his father.
Stephen		*[Rising]* Mnumzana, if dead streams can come back to life, it is my prayer that this valley can one day too, so that our children do not have to go away any more.
James		Yes, but how are we going to keep them here?
Stephen		By caring for our land before it is too late. I have spoken to the chief and to the headmaster about the restoration of Ndotsheni. The headmaster gives lectures. But he is unable to do anything. The chief and his counsellors, all they can do is frown, yet they know what must be done. But they cannot do it. *[He sits alongside **James**.]* All they say is that they will speak to the magistrate. And there it ends. So, I am left to pray.
James		*[He has made a conscious decision.]* I hear you, mfundisi, and I am grateful to you. *[**Stephen** frowns.]* For your kindness. For letting me speak of my pain in the midst of your own. Stay well, umfundisi.

*The thunder begins again as **James** sets off home. **Margaret**, no longer in mourning, re-appears up at the top. When he gets there, **James** embraces her and holds her.*

***Villagers**, wrapped up against the storm, run on.*

Actor 6	Carisbrooke is full of gossip. They say the Jarvises have gone quite mad. That if they go on with what they are planning to do, they will go broke.
Actor 4	But what are they going to do?
Actor 7	There's another storm coming. The fields are all in shadow. The thunder comes again.
Actor 6	The valley is very dark.
Actor 10	Lightning will strike soon.

Actor 7	And the wind will whirl the dust over the fields ...
Actor 6	It is very dark.
Actor 10	The drought must be breaking!
	The storm abates.
Actor 6	It is rumoured that a dam is to be built here, alongside the church, but no one knows how it will be filled, because the small stream that runs past the church has never been a great one at any time.
Actor 11	It's no rumour. There is to be a dam.
Actor 4	Mnumzana, where is the water to come from?
Actor 11	The water will come in a pipe from the river at High Place so that the cattle at Ndotsheni will always have water to drink. And the water from the dam will be let out at the gate, so it can water this land and that land ... the pastures that are planted ...
Actor 4	Jarvis has gone away to Pretoria. His business will surely be the business of the dam. Huh?
Actor 11	So the days pass. The sun rises and sets regularly over the earth. Kuluse's child recovers and Stephen goes about his pastoral duties.
Actor 7	Are the rumours of the dam true, he wonders? And more and more he finds himself thinking that if it is, if this one thing is true, that this could be the miracle he has been praying for. The miracle that would restore Ndotsheni to the land it was once before.
	Up at the top, **James** *appears with* **Napoleon Letsitsi** *[Actor 2]. They come down to the group of* **Villagers, Stephen,** *his* **Wife** *and the* **Girl.**
Actor 4	Hayi-bo *['Wow!'],* Jarvis is back!

*The **Villagers** sing a Zulu hymn of welcome and rejoicing.*

Actor 10   Not only did Jarvis return with the good news that the dam is to be built, he brought with him a learned man named Napoleon Letsitsi, an agricultural demonstrator, or farming officer, to work and live with them.

*The hymn of rejoicing explodes again and ends. **James** moves off to sit up above the **Villagers**. The **Villagers** settle down.*

SCENE 14

The Indaba.

Napoleon   From now on we must stop ploughing up and down the hills. We must plough around the hills.

Actor 4   No more up and down?

Napoleon   No more.

Actor 4   Awu!

Actor 6   But then the fields will no longer look like what they used to look like in the old days of ploughing.

Girl   Is that what the farming officer is telling us?

Napoleon   Yes, I am.

Actor 4   It is right. I work for uJarvis and uJarvis says it is right.

Actor 6   Awu, if Jarvis says it is right, then we will plough around the hills.

Napoleon   And we must throw away all the maize that we've kept for planting.

Rumbles of discontent.

Napoleon   I have better seed from uJarvis.

Actor 6	That we will take.
Wife	Uh-uh, we won't throw them away, we will eat them.
Actor 6	But what I want the farming officer to know is that the dam will eat up my land. And I do not like the land that I have been given in return. It is poor land.
	Napoleon is at his wits' end. Stephen steps in.
Stephen	Kuluse, when the dam is here there will be water, and when there is water, there will be grass, and when there is grass, there will be milk.
Actor 6	Yebo, baba umfundisi, I cannot refuse you. Through you came the milk that saved my child. Siyabonga, mfundisi.
Stephen	Siyabonga.
Napoleon	When the dam is made, there will be water for the pastures. I tell you there will be milk in this valley. It will not be necessary to take the white man's milk.
Stephen	Where would we be without the white man's milk? Where would we be without all that this white man has done for us?
Napoleon	Mfundisi, it was the white men who gave us so little land. It was white men that took us away from the land to go to work. And we were ignorant also. It is all these things together that have made this valley desolate. Therefore, what Mr Jarvis does is only repayment.
Stephen	Cha, cha, cha *['No, no, no']*, I do not like this talk.
Napoleon	I am sorry, mfundisi.
Stephen	No, you need not be sorry. I see you have a love for truth.
Napoleon	There is not even good farming without the truth. I also know that we do not work for men, that we work for the land and the people. We do not even work for money. *[Excited.]* We

	work for Africa, not for this man or that man. Not for a white man or a black man, but for Africa.
Stephen	Why do you not say South Africa?
Napoleon	*[Soberly]* We would if we could. *[He reflects for a moment.]* So, we speak as we sing, for we sing Nkosi Sikelel' iAfrika. You must not misunderstand me, mfundisi, I am not a man for politics. I am not a man to make trouble in your valley. I desire to restore it, that is all.
Actor 7	He is right! Napoleon is right!

*The hymn of rejoicing begins again as the **Villagers** descend on **Napoleon**, shaking his hand. Then suddenly they hoist him onto their shoulders. This unnerves him, he calls to be set down, hands and arms flailing wildly, as he is taken off.*

***Stephen** and **James** are left, laughing.*

• •

SCENE 15

	Evening.
James	It is the wish of my wife that I ask you this question. Do you desire a new church?
Stephen	*[Dumbstruck again.]* Awu, awu, awu, awu, awu …
James	The plans will shortly be with you, and you must say if they are what you desire.
Stephen	This is from God. This is from God.
James	My wife and I, we … we do all this in memory of our son.
Stephen	Ngiyabonga, mnumzana. Ngibonga ngomlimi, uyingilosi kaNkulunkulu. Ngibonga ngedamu. Manje ngibonga nangesonto. *['Thank you, sir. For the young agricultural*

demonstrator. He is an angel from God. I thank you for the dam. And now I thank you for the church too.']

James   Ngiyakuzwa. I came to you now, not because of the new church nor the memory of my son. Throughout this night, mfundisi, stay well.

James leaves.

Stephen   *[To the audience]* For this is the night of the fourteenth day.

A sombre and beautiful Zulu hymn begins.

*Stephen's **Wife** and the **Girl** come to him. His **Wife** gives him a bottle of tea and some cakes of maize wrapped up and a blanket. The **Girl** gives him his walking-stick and places his hat on his head.*

Stephen *climbs the mountain. He reaches a rock and sits down, putting the blanket around himself.*

*Up above, there appear **Absalom**, hands bound; **Theophilus**; **Father Vincent** in surplice, and a **Prison Official**. Absalom stands underneath the street lamp that could be mistaken for a gallows.*

*All the others keep vigil too. **Father Vincent** steps forward. As he describes things, **Stephen** does the actions.*

Vincent   And on the night of the fourteenth day when he comes to the place of the vigil on the mountain, it is cold. High on that mountaintop Stephen sits, unwraps the maize cakes from their cloth and places them with the tea on the stone. He gives thanks. Breaks the maize cake and eats of it and drinks of the tea.

***Theophilus**, up above, prayer book in hand, reading from it. **Father Vincent** returns to the place of execution.*

Light changes from dark to light as dawn approaches.

*On the mountain top, **James** approaches the place quietly.*

ACT 2   SCENE 15

Stephen	Absalom, my son!

*The priests make the sign of the cross as the **Prison Official** places a black hood over **Absalom's** head.*

*The **Contemporary Schoolboy** watches the two fathers.*

Lights fade onstage. The hymn stops.

• •

SCENE 16

Video footage of Alan Paton.

Alan Paton	I will now read the concluding paragraph of the book.

'Yes, it is the dawn that has come. The titihoya wakes from sleep, and goes about its work of forlorn crying. The sun tips with light the mountaintops of Ingeli and East Griqualand. The great valley of Umzimkulu is still in darkness, but the light will come there. Ndotsheni is still in darkness, but the light will come there also. For it is the dawn that has come, as it has come for a thousand centuries, never failing. But when that dawn will come, of our emancipation, from the fear of bondage and the bondage of fear, why that is a secret.'

Fade out.

GLOSSARY

Amanzi	Water
Amaphoyisa	Policeman
Awu	(*Hau*) Expression of sadness, disbelief or commiseration.
Ayikona	'No': an exclamation of disapproval similar to the modern English phrase 'No way'.
Baba	Father; Mister; Sir
Bafundisi	Teacher; priest; pastor
Diepkloof	A prison near Johannesburg.
Doornfontein	A suburb of Johannesburg.
Drakensberg	A wide mountainous region of South Africa.
East Griqualand	A region of South Africa which is included within the province of KwaZulu-Natal of South Africa.
Heavy	Serious
Hemu-hemu	A village located East of Pietermaritzburg in the province of KwaZulu-Natal, South Africa.
I-Afrika	Africa
Indaba	Village council
Ingeli	A forest located in the region of KwaZulu-Natal, South Africa.
Inkosikazi	Married woman
Isithuthuthu	Motorbike
Ixopo	A town situated in the province of KwaZulu-Natal, South Africa.
Ja	Yes
Jacarandas	A purple flowering tree common in parts of South Africa.

Kloofs	Mountains
Kontakion	Hymn
Kumalo	Stephen's family name.
Lufafa	A village located in the Eastern Cape of South Africa.
Mfowethu	Brother
Mfundisi/Umfundisi/ umnumzana	Reverend, priest, teacher – note that the first vowel u of these words is not sounded when used to address someone and in the first instance the final 'i' is whispered.
Mooi	A river that runs through the eastern province of KwaZulu-Natal in South Africa.
Natal	Former name of the province of KwaZulu-Natal in South Africa.
Ndotsheni	A remote village situated in the KwaZulu-Natal province of South Africa, where Stephen Kumalo lives with his wife.
Ngiyabonga	Thank you
Ngiyakuzwa	I hear you
Nihambe kahle	Go well
Nisale kahle	Keep well
Nkosana	Eldest son; prince
Nkosi Sikelel i-Afrika	A song, now part of South Africa's national anthem. It was considered the unofficial anthem during apartheid. The title of the song means 'God Bless Africa'.
Ntombazana	Girl
Pietermaritzburg	A town in KwaZulu-Natal in South Africa.
Pro deo	A phrase from Latin meaning 'for God'.
Siyabonga	Thank you

Titihoya	An African wading bird with a short pointed beak and black wings. The name represents the Zulu impression of the sound of the bird's call.
Transvaal	Former Gauteng region in South Africa.
Ubisi	Milk
Uhambe kahle	Go well
uJarvis	James Jarvis, Arthur's father.
Umkomaas	A town situated in the province of KwaZulu-Natal on the south coast of South Africa.
Umsundusi	A town located in the province of KwaZulu-Natal, south of the border of Mozambique and East of Swaziland.
Umuthi	Tree; medicine
Umzimkulu	A town situated in the eastern region of South Africa on the banks of the Umzimkulu River.
Unkosikazi wakhe	'His wife'
uNkulunkulu / Nkulunkulu	Great Spirit, or God
veld	Grassland
Volksrust	A town in the Mpumalanga province in South Africa.
Xhosa	A language spoken in South Africa, the Xhosa people are people who speak this language. It is most popularly spoken throughout the southern part of the country.
Yebo	Yes

ACTIVITIES

HISTORICAL SETTING	109
PROTESTS AND BOYCOTTS	112
WRITING A NEWSPAPER ARTICLE	115
LANDSCAPE AND MOOD	117
DEBATE – GUILTY OR INNOCENT?	120
A HERO	123
MIME QUIZ	126
FURTHER ACTIVITIES	128

Framework Substrand	Activities						
	1	2	3	4	5	6	7
1.1 Developing active listening skills and strategies		✓		✓	✓	✓	✓
1.2 Understanding and responding to what speakers say in formal and informal contexts							
2.1 Developing and adapting speaking skills and strategies in formal and informal contexts		✓			✓		
2.2 Using and adapting the conventions and forms of spoken texts							
3.1 Developing and adapting discussion skills and strategies in formal and informal contexts		✓			✓		
3.2 Taking roles in group discussion		✓			✓		
4.1 Using different dramatic approaches to explore ideas, texts and issues		✓			✓		✓
4.2 Developing, adapting and responding to dramatic techniques, conventions and styles		✓			✓		✓
5.1 Developing and adapting active reading skills and strategies	✓	✓	✓	✓	✓	✓	✓
5.2 Understanding and responding to ideas, viewpoints, themes and purposes in texts				✓		✓	✓
5.3 Reading and engaging with a wide and varied range of texts							
6.1 Relating texts to the social, historical and cultural contexts in which they were written	✓			✓	✓		✓
6.2 Analysing how writers' use of linguistic and literary features shapes and influences writing				✓			
6.3 Analysing writers' use of organization, structure, layout and presentation	✓			✓			
7.1 Generating ideas, planning and drafting	✓	✓	✓		✓		✓
7.2 Using and adapting the conventions and forms of texts on paper and screen							
8.1 Developing viewpoint, voice and ideas		✓	✓		✓		
8.2 Varying sentences and punctuation for clarity and effect	✓	✓	✓	✓			
8.3 Improving vocabulary for precision and impact	✓	✓	✓	✓			
8.4 Developing varied linguistic and literary techniques		✓	✓	✓			
8.5 Structuring, organizing and presenting texts in a variety of forms on paper and on screen		✓	✓			✓	
8.6 Developing and using editing and proofreading skills on paper and on screen		✓	✓				
9.1 Using the conventions of standard English							
9.2 Using grammar accurately and appropriately		✓	✓	✓			
9.3 Reviewing spelling and increasing knowledge of word derivations, patterns and families			✓				
10.1 Exploring language variation and development according to time, place, culture, society and technology		✓	✓				
10.2 Commenting on language use							

HISTORICAL SETTING

The novel, *Cry, the Beloved Country*, was written by Alan Paton and published in 1948. It soon became an international best seller. The novel focused on the problem of race relations in South Africa, where a minority of white people held power over the majority of non-white people, including Blacks, Indians and Coloureds (people of mixed race).

VOCABULARY CHECK

Minority – the smallest part of a group of people or things

Majority – the greatest part of a group of people or things

MAKING A TIME LINE

The panels below give a short history of South Africa, but they are in the wrong order. Read them carefully and put them in the correct order on a time line, starting with number 1.

> For thousands of years (before written history) tribes of hunter-gatherers, farmers and traders lived in South Africa.

> In 1923, non-whites were forbidden to live in the same parts of town as the whites.

> In the 17th century, Dutch settlers came to South Africa. They became known as Afrikaners.

> In 1913 non-whites were forbidden to own land except in special 'reserve' areas.

In 1948 the government passed a series of laws to separate the races further. The system became known as 'apartheid'. It meant that non-white people could not vote, they could not work, live, travel or even be educated where they wanted.

In 1927 mixed marriages between different races were forbidden.

In 1810 South Africa became part of the British Empire. Many British people came to live there.

In the mid 19th century, gold and diamonds were discovered in South Africa. The white people took control of the mines.

In 1910 a new group of laws gave more power to the whites and took away many freedoms from non-whites.

ASSESSMENT

- **Self-assessment**. Rate your success with this task on a scale of 1 to 5, with 5 being the highest.
- Give yourself a bonus mark if you understood that all dates in a named century, begin with the two numbers of the previous century, for example, all years in the 19th century begin 18xx.

RESEARCH

Do some research in pairs or small groups to continue the time line to bring it up to date.
- Divide the tasks so that each pair or group research at least one event.
- Look up information on the Internet and in books. Make a note of dates, key names and what happened.

- Write a short, clear summary of the event. Remember to write in standard English and to include facts rather than opinions.
- Present your event to the rest of the group or class and position it on the time line. Be prepared to talk about *why* the event was significant in the history of South Africa, as well as what actually happened.

Possible events to research:
- the eviction from Sophiatown, 1955
- the Sharpville massacre, 1960
- the trial of Nelson Mandela, 1962
- the Soweto riots, 1976
- the death of Steve Biko, 1977
- international sanctions, 1980s
- the release of Nelson Mandela, 1990
- the first democratic general election, 1944.

ASSESSMENT

- **Peer assessment**. Swap your summary with another group or pair. Ask them to comment on how clear your summary is and whether they can make it more concise (shorter) without losing any key information.
- **Teacher assessment**. Your teacher will check that all events in the time line are sequenced in chronological order. He or she should also assess how accurate your explanation was of the significance of your chosen event in the history of South Africa.

PROTESTS AND BOYCOTTS

Re-read Act 1 Scene 13. In a small group, imagine that this protest is part of a wider campaign to draw attention to the increasing divisions in society. Your group is to plan this campaign. Follow the steps below:

In your group, draw up a list of all things that you feel are unfair about apartheid. You might consider things like housing, education, transport, voting, etc.

Decide how you will get public attention, e.g. through posters, leaflets, talking to journalists, giving TV interviews and making public protests and speeches.

Think up some slogans for your cause. They should be short, memorable and easy to chant. Try to use alliteration, repetition, rhyme or a pattern of three for maximum effect.

VOCABULARY CHECK

Alliteration is the repetition of the first sound of words, e.g. *Fight for freedom!*

Rhyme is a similar sound in the endings of words, e.g. *A shilling is killing!*

Allocate tasks to members of your group. For example, one person could draw up a poster, another couple could write a leaflet; someone else could write to a newspaper, someone else could write a short public speech to deliver at the bus boycott.

Work on your individual tasks then share the results with the rest of your group. Make two positive comments about each task and suggest one way of making an improvement.

Make a final draft of your work then present it to your class.

Remember
All protest is against the law, so your work is dangerous. You are fighting for basic freedoms, so make sure your message is clear and strong!

ASSESSMENT

- **Peer assessment.** Ask your group to assess how well you contributed to the group's work: very well, quite well, could have done more.
- **Self assessment.** Tick the things in this list that you think you did well and think about how you might do the others better next time:
  - listened carefully to others
  - contributed ideas to the group
  - produced a good piece of written or spoken work that was appropriate to the target audience.

IMPROVISING A SCENE

Act out another short scene at the bus boycott. Divide the roles into:
- protesters
- black people who have turned up to take the bus
- white people who are taking the bus.

Each group should work together to prepare their roles. Think carefully about why they are there, how they are feeling, how they might speak and behave, and how they might interact with the other groups.

Note that not everyone in the same group needs to share the same ideas. For example, some black people might feel they have to take the bus because they are too frail to walk the eleven miles, even though they would like to support the boycott. Some white people might sympathize with the protesters while others fear them.

When you are ready, enact the scene. One person should be the bus driver, deciding when the bus arrives, how long it stops for and when it drives off.

ASSESSMENT

- **Self assessment**. Give yourself marks out of ten for how well you did in your role. Think carefully about whether you really 'became' another character and behaved accordingly.
- **Peer assessment**. As a group, decide which character was most convincing and why.

WRITING A NEWSPAPER ARTICLE

In Act 1, Scene 19 a newspaper seller is shouting:

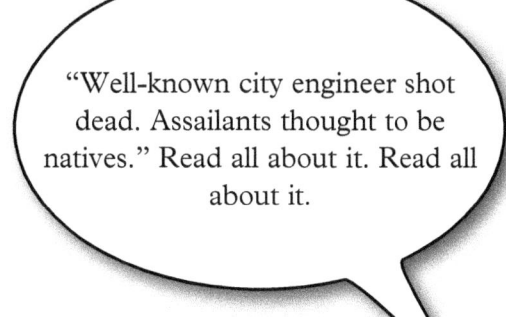

> "Well-known city engineer shot dead. Assailants thought to be natives." Read all about it. Read all about it.

Your task is to write that newspaper article, which is about the murder of Arthur Jarvis. Follow the steps below.

1. Re-read Scene 18 to remind yourself of the sequence of events.
2. Re-read Scene 16 and think carefully about the response of the white people to crime. Note that the majority would have agreed with Mr De Villiers, although some, like Arthur Jarvis himself, saw the complexity of the situation and felt the problem was deeply rooted in the unfair segregation of society.
3. Imagine that your newspaper is read mainly by whites, but as a journalist you feel you must give different viewpoints. So, include some quotations from both Mr De Villiers and Father Vincent, commenting on the murder.
4. You will need to think up a suitable headline – something short and attention-grabbing.
5. Introduce the story stating where, what, when, why and who.

6 Give some background information about Arthur Jarvis and his work.
7 Include quotations from (imaginary) interviews with people commenting on the crime.
8 End your article with a thought about the consequences of this crime and possibly a question for your reader.
9 You may wish to include a picture and a caption to accompany your text.
10 Check through your article carefully:
- ensure that you have used topic sentences to introduce each paragraph
- check your spelling and punctuation.

ASSESSMENT

- **Self assessment.** Decide which of the following you found most difficult and think about how you might improve next time:
  - thinking up a headline
  - structuring your content
  - writing in paragraphs with topic sentences
  - including quotations from interviews
  - writing in standard English, appropriate for a newspaper.
- **Teacher assessment.** Focus on some sample articles, highlighting the most effective aspects of each, and explaining why and how they are effective.

LANDSCAPE AND MOOD

One of Alan Paton's publishers commented that 'one of the most important characters in the book is the land of South Africa itself'. The descriptions of the countryside and towns weave through the novel and often reflect the mood of the story.

This is an extract from the first chapter of the novel:

> Where you stand the grass is rich and matted, you cannot see the soil. But the rich green hills break down. They fall to the valley below, and falling, change their nature. For they grow red and bare; they cannot hold the rain and mist, and the streams are dry in the kloofs. Too many cattle feed upon the grass, and too many fires have burned it. Stand shod upon it, for it is coarse and sharp, and the stones cut under the feet. It is not kept, or guarded, or cared for, it no longer keeps men, guards men, cares for men. The titihoya does not cry here any more.
>
> The great red hills stand desolate, and the earth has torn away like flesh. The lightning flashes over them, the clouds pour down upon them, the dead streams come to life, full of the red blood of the earth. Down in the valleys women scratch the soil that is left, and the maize hardly reaches the height of a man . . .

The author is portraying a bleak landscape. It has been exploited and is now hostile. Even the native bird (the titihoya) no longer sings there.

Look carefully at the language the author uses and how it conveys such a powerful image. Pick out the following features:

- personification of the hills (i.e. when the hills are given human qualities)
- repetition
- pattern of three
- a simile (where something is compared to another with the use of the word 'like' or 'as')
- a metaphor (where something is said to *be* something else)
- emotive words (linked to injury or death).

In the playscript, this description is relayed by a series of actors. It explains why country people moved to the cities to find work but also gives the overall impression of a country that is damaged and a people that are suffering. This echoes the wider message of the book about the divisions and devastation of society.

ENDING

This is the final paragraph of both the novel and playscript:

> Yes, it is the dawn that has come. The titihoya wakes from sleep, and goes about its work of forlorn crying. The sun tips with light the mountaintops of Ingeli and East Griqualand. The great valley of Umzimkulu is still in darkness, but the light will come there. Ndotsheni is still in darkness, but the light will come there also. For it is the dawn that has come, as it has come for a thousand centuries, never failing. But when that dawn will come, of our emancipation, from the fear of bondage and the bondage of fear, why that is a secret.

Think carefully about how the writer is using images of the landscape to convey a deeper message. Discuss the questions below.

1. What is the overall image that is built up in the reader's mind? (Think about the time of day.)

2   Is it a static (still) image, or a progressive (changing) one?
3   How might that image relate to what was happening in South African society?
4   Do you think the author was optimistic or pessimistic for the future of South Africa?

WRITING CHALLENGE

Write a descriptive paragraph, in which a natural event or landscape reflects the mood or action of people. Here are some possible ideas:
- two people are arguing while a storm rages outside
- a lonely man or woman gets lost in a desert
- an animal dies in the late evening
- a new friendship begins in spring.

ASSESSMENT

- **Self assessment**. Think carefully about your understanding of how authors use descriptions of the natural world to echo the events and mood of characters. Decide whether your understanding is good, quite good or not good.
- **Peer assessment**. Swap your descriptive paragraph with another student. Give two positive comments and one comment about an area that could be improved.

DEBATE - GUILTY OR INNOCENT?

In Act 2, Scene 7 the Judge pronounces sentence on Absalom: 'I sentence you, Absalom Kumalo, to be returned to custody, and to be hanged by the neck until you are dead. And may the Lord have mercy on your soul.' This is followed by a Zulu hymn of mourning.

Discuss why a hymn of mourning would be sung for the death of a murderer.

Although Absalom did shoot Arthur Jarvis, his punishment is controversial. Hold another trial for Absalom in the classroom.

- Divide into two groups: one group should be the prosecution (i.e. accuse Absalom of being guilty and demand his death), the other group should be the defence (i.e. claim that Absalom should be either freed or imprisoned, rather than hanged).
- Each group should prepare their case. Consider the following:
    - Did Absalom mean to kill Arthur Jarvis?
    - Was it Absalom's idea to take the gun?
    - Are people always responsible for their own actions?
    - Should Matthew Kumalo take some responsibility?
    - Would Absalom have turned to crime if he had been given a good education and found a good job, like a white person in South Africa?
    - Is it important to see justice being done?
    - What would be the effect of the hanging of Absalom on his family, friends, home tribe and the white community?
- Skim the playscript for quotations that could be used at the trial. Make a note of them.

'It is not easy being born a South African' (Arthur Jarvis, Act 2, Scene 3)

'I hope to God they string them up!' (James Jarvis, Act 2, Scene 5)

'I plead guilty to killing, but I did not mean to kill.' (Absalom, Act 2, Scene 5)

'We must demand more protection. More police. Heavier sentences.' Mr De Villiers, Act 1, Scene 21)

'We will always have native crime to fear until the native people of this country are given worthy purposes to inspire them and worthy goals to work for.' (Arthur Jarvis, Act 1, Scene 16)

- One member of the defence group should volunteer to be Absalom at the trial. He or she should stand at the front of the class and answer all questions in role.
- A spokesperson from the prosecution should put forward the group's views and questions.
- A spokesperson from the defence should put forward the group's views and questions.
- A judge (the teacher or a pupil) sums up the arguments for and against Absalom.
- The whole class act as a jury and vote on whether Absalom is innocent or guilty and what type of punishment (if any) he should be given.

ASSESSMENT

- **Self assessment.** Rate your performance on a scale of 1 to 5 (5 being the highest score) for the following:
  - contributing ideas to the group
  - listening carefully to others
  - staying in a character role (if relevant).
- **Teacher assessment.** Ask your teacher to pick out one of the best aspects of the debate on both sides. Also ask him or her to highlight an area that could be improved upon.

A HERO

- In pairs, talk about what you understand by the term 'hero' (Note that this term can be applied to both men and women.)
- Jot down your ideas and share them with another couple.
- Write a definition of the term and give some examples. Use a dictionary to give you more ideas, but make sure the definition is your own.
- According to your definition, would you regard Arthur Jarvis as a hero?

Arthur Jarvis was brave, intelligent and compassionate. He stepped outside his comfortable life to make his own decisions about the society he lived in. Most of his white contemporaries were happy to just enjoy their lives of privilege. They were willing to accept the (misguided) view that non-whites were inferior and therefore did not deserve the same rights, freedom and power as the whites.

Skim read the playscript to find where we learn about Arthur Jarvis, his views and the impact had on people. Note that some of his actions spoke as loudly as his words. Make notes about what each incident reveals about him and his views, then copy and complete the grid on the following page.

Place in script	Quotation, action or event	What this reveals
Act 1, Scene 14	Arthur gives Theophilus and Stephen a lift, even though it is out of his way.	
	'The good things of Alexandra are more than the bad . . .'	
Act 1, Scene 16		
Act 2, Scene 3		
Act 2, Scene 5	At his funeral the church was too small for all who wanted to come . . .	

CHARACTER PROFILE

Imagine you are Arthur Jarvis and you are joining a social networking site. Plan what you might put on your site. Think carefully about:
- friends to include and how you met them
- what you like
- what you dislike
- your job
- messages that you might post on your site
- messages that other characters might post on your 'wall'. (For example, comments from your mum, dad, Mr De Villiers, Theophilus, etc. Make sure their messages are in keeping with what you know about these individual characters' viewpoints.)

ASSESSMENT

- **Self assessment**. How well do you feel you understand the character of Arthur Jarvis? Very well, quite well, or not well at all?
- **Peer assessment**. Swap your plans for the social networking site with a partner. Ask them to rate it on a scale of 1 to 5 (5 being the highest score) according to how well it shows Arthur Jarvis's character. Ask them to add their own comment to the 'wall' in the role of another character.

MIME QUIZ

This class quiz is to test your knowledge of the play and your understanding of the characters' feelings.
- In pairs, select a few short extracts from the playscript.
- Decide on which two characters to play.
- Rehearse how you might enact the extract, but in *mime*, i.e. without speaking. You will need to focus on your facial expressions, body language and gestures. Also think carefully about how you interact with the other character.
- When all pairs have had time to rehearse, come together as a class.
- Take it in turns to enact your scene. During this enactment a member of the audience may tap you on the shoulder at any time. When this happens both of you must 'freeze'. The actor who has been tapped then has to say what he or she is *feeling* (note, <u>not</u> what he or she is doing).
- The class must guess the correct scene and the characters that you and your partner are playing.

Here are some scenes that you might consider:
- Stephen at the bus stop, being cheated out of his money by the young man
- the brothers meet at John Kumalo's carpentry shop
- the murder of Arthur Jarvis
- the bus boycott
- the execution of Absalom
- the funeral of Arthur Jarvis
- the marriage of the girl and Absalom
- the son of Jarvis and Stephen meet in the church.

ASSESSMENT

- **Peer assessment.** Ask the class which couple enacted their scene most effectively in mime. Encourage them to give a specific reason why they felt it was most effective.
- **Teacher assessment.** Preview the rehearsals, giving advice to pairs on how they might improve their presentation, but also praising their strengths.

FURTHER ACTIVITIES

1. Write a diary entry that Absalom could have written the night before his execution. Reflect on what he has done and how he feels about himself and others. Remember to use the first person.
2. Discuss the use of symbols in the playscript. For example, the doll's house, the toy car and train, the veil.
3. Write some more of the essay that Arthur Jarvis was writing when he was shot. Think carefully about the essay title and what he may have been intending to write about: 'A private essay on the evolution of a South African'.
4. Make a list of all the sounds that are required for a performance of the playscript, e.g. jazz in the township, bird cry, thunder, hymns, songs of mourning. Compile a recording of as many of these sounds as you can.
5. Do some research into Alan Paton's life and work. How much do you think they influenced each other?